More Praise for *Hello, My Name Is Awesome*

"This awesome piece of writing is worth bottling, shaking, and stirring into your brand-name strategy either online or offline. I love the way Alexandra weaves her voice and humor into a very clear message to distill what you are about into a business name. It can be applied to your brand name and domain name. Her process is coherent and creative. A brilliant book I couldn't put down."

—**Jeff Bullas, blogger, strategist, and speaker,** *Forbes* **Top 50 Social Media Power Influencer 2013, and** *Huffington Post* **Top 100 Business Twitter Account**

"I was skeptical about a how-to book on naming products and brands. Alexandra Watkins convinced me otherwise. Her book is a fun read with lots of practical advice."

—**Patricia Roller, angel investor and former Co-CEO, Frog Design**

"Your company or product probably needs all the help it can get. Watkins helped me name my firm, and I'm constantly told what a great name it is. Don't pick a name until you've read Watkins's book—you'll want to have a name that you love forever!"

—**Charlene Li, founder of Altimeter Group, author of** *Open Leadership*, **and coauthor of** *Groundswell*

"The type of hands-on practical wisdom rarely found (but desperately needed) in the academic community."

—**Michael Webber, Dean of the School of Management, University of San Francisco**

"This is the perfect book for kick-starting entrepreneurs, brand managers, and practicing creatives."

—**Pat Hanlon, founder and CEO, Thinktopia, and author of** *Primal Branding*

"This book is packed full of practical, real-world advice you would never get from a regular textbook."

—**Dale J. Stephens, founder of UnCollege and author of** *Hacking Your Education*

"In the current crazy business climate, where standing out and being remembered are critical to success, your name had better be awesome. This is the best book on the subject."

—**Nell Merlino, founder and President, Count Me In for Women's Economic Independence, and creator of Take Our Daughters to Work Day**

"We've got a terrible name. No one can spell it. No one can pronounce it. Don't make the same mistake we made. Read this book and let Alexandra Watkins guide you away from the 'we thought we were being clever with our name, but now we just look silly' syndrome."

—**Matt Ruby, founder and CEO, Vooza**

Hello, My Name Is

AWESOME

How to Create Brand Names That Stick

ALEXANDRA WATKINS

BK

Berrett–Koehler Publishers, Inc.
San Francisco
a BK Business book

JAN 1 5 2015

Berrett-Koehler Publishers, Inc.
235 Montgomery Street, Suite 650
San Francisco, CA 94104-2916
Tel: (415) 288-0260   Fax: (415) 362-2512   www.bkconnection.com

Ordering Information

Quantity sales. Special discounts are available on quantity purchases by corporations, associations, and others. For details, contact the "Special Sales Department" at the Berrett-Koehler address above.

Individual sales. Berrett-Koehler publications are available through most bookstores. They can also be ordered directly from Berrett-Koehler:
Tel: (800) 929-2929; Fax: (802) 864-7626; www.bkconnection.com.

Orders for college textbook/course adoption use. Please contact Berrett-Koehler:
Tel: (800) 929-2929; Fax: (802) 864-7626.

Orders by U.S. trade bookstores and wholesalers. Please contact Ingram Publisher Services, Tel: (800) 509-4887; Fax: (800) 838-1149; E-mail: customer.service@ingrampublisherservices.com; or visit www.ingrampublisherservices.com/Ordering for details about electronic ordering.

Berrett-Koehler and the BK logo are registered trademarks of Berrett-Koehler Publishers, Inc.

Printed in the United States of America

Berrett-Koehler books are printed on long-lasting acid-free paper. When it is available, we choose paper that has been manufactured by environmentally responsible processes. These may include using trees grown in sustainable forests, incorporating recycled paper, minimizing chlorine in bleaching, or recycling the energy produced at the paper mill.

Library of Congress Cataloging-in-Publication Data

Watkins, Alexandra.
Hello, my name is awesome : how to create brand names that stick / Alexandra Watkins.
    pages   cm
ISBN 978-1-62656-186-1 (paperback)
    1. Branding (Marketing)   2. Bralnd name products.   I. Title.
HF5415.1255.W38   2014
658.8'27—dc23   2014018994

First Edition

18   17   16   15   14   10 9 8 7 6 5 4 3 2 1

Book producer and text designer: BookMatters, Berkeley, CA
Copyeditor: Tanya Grove
Proofreader: Nancy Evans
Indexer: Leonard Rosenbaum
Cover designer: Tracy Moon/StudioMoon Visual Identity

430 8546

To my awesome mother, Joan Casale.

Thank you for being there
for every chapter of my life,
and every page of this book.

The meaning of life is to find your gift.
The purpose of life is to give it away.

—Pablo Picasso

CONTENTS

PREFACE

Whether people see it on your storefront, read it on your badge at a trade show, or see it on their caller ID, your brand name makes a critical first impression. Even more than your shoes.

I wrote this book to show how anyone, even the most non-creative person, can come up with awesome brand names and have fun doing it.

Creating names is not a science. Yet naming firms spout ridiculous jargon about "verbal identity engineering," "rigorous methodologies," "computational linguistics," and "scientific scrutiny applied to the unstructured and undisciplined process of brand name creation." Others try to invent names using math. They take a completely fine word, crunch it with another word, and get a name that doesn't compute. Or, they subtract a few letters from a perfectly good word and end up with a random name that looks like it was made from the miscellaneous Scrabble tiles left at the end of a game.

Does any of that sound even remotely creative?

Consumers don't fall in love with brand names created by scientific processes, linguistic voodoo, or mangling the alphabet. Those kinds of names don't resonate with us because they don't make emotional connections.

The most powerful brand names connect with people and move them to buy because they are based on familiar words and concepts that they understand and appreciate: Kryptonite locks, Mayday tech support, Obsession perfume, Leap Frog toys, Ninja blender—these are the names that speak volumes.

As an advertising copywriter at Ogilvy & Mather, I learned the art of making emotional connections with words. Years later, I began creating names and discovered that, just as a clever print ad headline will turn heads, generate buzz, and spark sales, brand names can have those same magical powers.

I am going to give you my bag of tricks.

INTRODUCTION

"Hello, my name is Alexandra." Sounds simple enough. But people often butcher my name: "Alexandria," Alexandrea," "Alexia." And much to my annoyance, the 100 percent male version, "Alexander."

What about your first and last names? Are they tricky to spell? Difficult to pronounce? Hard for people to remember? This trifecta of trouble is rampant among brand names: Sur La Table, Iams, Flickr, Saucony, Eukanuba, Xobni. Those are just a handful of head scratchers that consumers struggle with. But unlike the name you were born with, or married into, these easily bungled names were intentionally created by companies. At the time, these businesses may have thought they were being clever. But even after being in business for years, these brands still have to explain, spell, pronounce, and apologize for their names.

I am going to prevent you from making the same mistakes.

As the founder of a nationally known naming firm, Eat My Words (www.eatmywords.com), I have spent nearly a decade creating names for everything from consumer electronics to cupcake stores. Clients including Disney, Microsoft, and Wrigley hire my firm because they have discovered what I have known for years—the kind of brand names that resonate the most with consumers are names that people *get* and like. We want to feel clever not clueless. (Have you figured out what Xobni is yet?)

I've packed this book with firsthand knowledge that will enlighten and entertain you. You won't find any junk science, branding jargon, or linguistic mumbo jumbo. And I haven't included the etymology of famous brand names. Sure, those stories are interesting. But this is a how-to guide, not a history book.

Instead, you will get practical, up-to-date advice, such as

making sure that Siri and voice recognition software spell your name correctly. You'll read never-before-heard stories of naming triumphs and train wrecks. And you'll see dozens and dozens of eye-opening name examples—the good, the bad, and the so-bad-I-gave them-an-award. I am not afraid to name names.

I break down the brainstorming process by walking you through how to come up with dozens of fantastic name ideas using the very same tools, techniques, and resources that I use every day.

My creative and fun techniques for coming up with names can be learned by anyone, even the most left-brained engineer. How is that possible? I don't use linguistics to create unfamiliar words. Instead, my approach is purely conceptual. It's based on what I've learned after spending more than twenty years as an advertising copywriter: clever ad headlines get noticed, get buzz, and get sales because they make strong emotional connections with consumers. Brand names can have that same effect.

Before we jump into brainstorming name ideas, you'll learn how to objectively evaluate names using the SMILE & SCRATCH test, a checklist based on my philosophy that a name should make you smile instead of scratch your head.

SMILE: The 5 Qualities of a Super-Sticky Name

Suggestive — evokes something about your brand

Meaningful — resonates with your audience

Imagery — is visually evocative to aid in memory

Legs — lends itself to a theme for extended mileage

Emotional — moves people

SCRATCH: The 7 Deadly Sins

Spelling challenged — looks like a typo

Copycat — is similar to competitors' names

Restrictive — limits future growth

Annoying — is forced or frustrates customers

Tame — is flat, descriptive, uninspired

Curse of Knowledge — makes sense only to insiders

Hard to pronounce — is not obvious or is unapproachable

This filter is kind of a no-brainer, right? Yet you'd be surprised how many brand names fail this test. (How does *Xobni* do?) Everything in this book is that simple.

And by the time you finish the last chapter, you will have everything you need to create awesome names on your own.

I'll admit that some of my colleagues think I'm crazy for sharing my secret sauce. They worry that I may cannibalize my business by showing "amateurs" how to do what I get paid the big bucks for. While I don't think the book will put me out of the name game, I do hope it will put me out of my misery by preventing more bad names from happening to good people.

Alexandra Watkins

P.S. If you haven't figured it out yet, Xobni is *in box* spelled backward. Just don't ask me how to pronounce it.

CHAPTER 1

The 5 Qualities of a Super-Sticky Name

How do you react when you see or hear a name you like? You smile. We enjoy names that surprise us, entertain us, and make us feel smart because we *get* them.

Names that make us smile are infectious. They are the ones we talk about, tweet, and repeat because we like other people to smile, too.

I love seeing the grin on someone's face when I say that I named a Spanish language school in Colombia *Gringo Lingo*. I get the same reaction when I mention the robotic vacuum I named Neato. And most people laugh out loud when they hear about the Church of Cupcakes.

Imagine if before people were even customers of yours, they

loved your product or company simply because they loved the name. Maybe they'd even pay to buy a T-shirt with the name on it. That's the power of a name that makes people smile.

Remember the philosophy that the SMILE & SCRATCH name evaluation test is based on: A name should make you smile instead of scratch your head. SMILE is an acronym for the five qualities of a great name, which I cover here. (SCRATCH is the flipside, which we look at in the next chapter.)

SMILE:
The 5 Qualities of a Super-Sticky Name

Suggestive

Meaningful

Imagery

Legs

Emotional

Ideally your name should have all of the above attributes.

Suggestive —
Evokes Something about Your Brand

A name can't be expected to say *everything*, but it should suggest something about your brand. Not in a descriptive way, like Fast Signs, but in a creative or metaphorical way, such as Amazon.

The name Amazon suggests *enormous*. Founder Jeff Bezos chose the name because, to him, Amazon conjured up images of one of the world's largest rivers, and he envisioned his company being unfathomably large.

While Amazon.com famously started as an online bookseller in 1994, the company expanded rapidly into other areas. By 1999 the company was selling music, consumer electronics, video games, software, home-improvement items, toys and games, and much more. Of course, now it offers everything from lingerie to lawnmowers. And Amazon drones may one day be delivering our packages. No matter what they do or sell in the future, the name *Amazon* will always fit. Can you imagine if it had been named BookBarn.com?

Suggestive Coined Names

I have great respect for anyone who can invent a clever name that suggests something about the brand. Some of my favorite coined names are Dreamery, Groupon, Pictionary, Cinnabon, Chillow, Pinterest, Chuggernaut, and San Franpsycho. These names, also known as *portmanteaus*, work well because they cleverly marry two words together, are intuitive to spell, and easy to pronounce. Easier said than done. (More on that in the next chapter.) Other coined names that work well are those that suggest a positive brand experience. Jamba Juice, Twizzlers, and Zappos all live up to their fun, high-energy names.

A Suggestive Name Can Be Inspired by Your Brand's Personality

When you write your *creative brief* (Chapter 4), you'll jot down a few adjectives that describe the personality of your brand. You can use those words to spark name ideas. For instance, if you want to convey that your brand is adventurous and rugged, think of metaphors and phrases that fit those words. SUV names do this incredibly well. Explorer, Expedition, Range Rover, Yukon, and Denali all suggest rugged adventure.

Ad agencies are notorious for suggesting creative prowess through their wonderfully strange names. Some of the most imaginative are Victors & Spoils, Captains of Industry, The Glue Society, and Wexley School for Girls. These are certainly more interesting than traditional agency names like Foote, Cone & Belding.

How to Suggest Trust or Credibility

While your business should certainly be trustworthy and credible, trying to cram any form of those words into your name can sound disingenuous. Luckily, there are many other ways you can convey that you have a quality company or product. Adding a strong secondary word in your name is an excellent solution. For instance, the company that makes the robotic vacuum Neato is named Neato Robotics. Other modifiers you can try are *Global*, *Industries*, or *Group*, which can instantly add heft to you name. Other ways to convey trust and credibility include customer testimonials on your website, a guarantee, professionally designed promotional materials, and an active social media presence. Actions speak louder than words.

MORE EXAMPLES OF SUGGESTIVE NAMES

Leaf (electric car)	Ninja (blender)
Kickstarter (crowdfunding)	FitBit (activity trackers)
Brawny (paper towels)	

Meaningful —
Resonates with Your Audience

It's important to make sure your name is meaningful to potential customers, not just to you. Most of the time when people encounter your name, you won't be there to explain it to them. And they won't have the time or interest to read about it on your website or the back of the box.

No one needs to explain the meaning of the name Norcal Waste Systems. It's unfortunately descriptive and has awful visual imagery. Not exactly something you would want to have emblazoned on a T-shirt or water bottle.

When the company was formed in 1983, the name Norcal Waste Systems was fine for the commercial businesses they served. But twenty-five years later, with hundreds of thousands of residential garbage-collection customers, the name was far from appealing. *Waste* had an especially negative meaning to the environmentally conscious communities it served in northern California, Oregon, and Washington. What these customers cared about was recycling, composting, and reclaiming useful materials before they were buried in a landfill. Ironically, Norcal Waste Systems was an industry leader in all of these areas. But no one would ever guess that based on the name.

In April 2009, Norcal Waste Systems changed its name to Recology, fusing the words *recycle* and *ecology*. This progressive new name evokes the company's environmental shift, resonates with both residential and commercial customers, and is a source of pride (instead of embarrassment) for their 2,100 employees.

A Meaningful Long Name Is Better than a Short Meaningless Name

It's better to have a meaningful name that people can remember than a meaningless name they can type in five keystrokes. The name of the online home furnishings store Previously Owned by a Gay Man is loaded with meaning and is much more memorable than a shortened version (PreOw) or its abbreviation (POBAGM).

The longest name I know of belonged to one of the entertainment law firms that represented Michael Jackson: Ziffren, Brittenham, Branca, Fischer, Gilbert-Lurie, Stiffelman, Cook, Johnson, Lande & Wolf. I'm not sure how meaningful such a long name could be to their clients, but until recently, when they shortened it to Ziffren Brittenham LLP, the names of all ten partners composed the name of this twenty-three-person firm. I would love to have seen how they crammed that onto a business card.

Do Not Name Your Company after Yourself

While it may evoke warm thoughts to your friends and family, your personal name is meaningless to your future customers. They don't know you yet. Your name evokes absolutely nothing about your business, expertise, or brand personality. And if you're like many of us, your name is either hard to spell, hard to pronounce, or hard for people to remember. Why would you want to have a business name with the same difficulties? (I suspect you know this, which is why you are reading this book.)

Unfortunately, most consultants and service professionals (architects, attorneys, photographers, professional speakers, etc.) use their own name by default because "That's what everyone else does." Most don't know any better, lack creative inspiration, or simply let their ego get in the way. This is a huge missed opportunity. Fortunately you are reading this book and won't make the same mistake.

Tejal Topiwala is a talented home stager and interior designer in Toronto. For most people in North America, her name is intimidating to pronounce. She had the foresight to know that it might be a barrier for people to pick up the phone and call if they were unsure how to pronounce her name. And of course her name wouldn't distinguish her in any way from her competitors. We branded her company *Paprika*, with the tagline "Spice up your space." This new identity recognizes her flair for color, lends itself to wordplay, has beautiful imagery, and is a fantastic conversation starter. And most of all, it lets prospective clients know that she's creative.

If Your Personal Name Lends Itself to Wordplay, Get Clever

If your first or last name lends itself to wordplay, you may be able to create a clever brand name out of it. Dawn Gluskin is a multimillion-dollar entrepreneur and coach who shares advice through her company, Dawnsense. Steven Lord is a consultant who calls his business Lord Knows!

If you do go this route, consider what could happen if you sell your company and your name is still attached to it, as happened to Shari Fitzpatrick, the founder of the original chocolate-dipped strawberry company, Shari's Berries. For two decades, Shari cultivated tens of thousands of loyal customers and a reputation for creating beautifully hand-dipped creations. Shari's Berries became well known, thanks to *O* Magazine, QVC, and the SkyMall catalog, where her product was featured on the cover three times. But after making a bad business decision,

Shari was pushed out of her own company. A large corporation now owns Shari's Berries and mass-produces a product that bears little resemblance to the original. It makes Shari cringe that anyone would ever associate her good name with an inferior product. There's nothing she can do about it. She is forbidden to use her own name for her new company. (She does have a cute new name, though—Berried In Chocolate—inspired by the title of her chocolate-covered book, which is quite delicious.)

MORE EXAMPLES OF MEANINGFUL NAMES

Kryptonite (bike locks)

Breakthrough (mental health website)

Repel (insect repellent)

Mayday (tech support button)

Yelp (customer reviews)

Imagery —
Visually Evocative to Aid in Memory

Think of people you've met throughout your life who have unusual first names. For me, that would be Daisy, Forest, and Chopper. I met all of them more than ten years ago during a six-week backpacking trip through New Zealand. (Chopper was a helicopter pilot.) I met dozens of people on my trip, but those three are the ones I remember instantly because the names have such strong associations with things that I can picture in my mind. That's the power of a visually evocative name.

Wouldn't you love to have a product or company name that would be so embedded in people's memories that they could recall it ten years later? You can, if you name your product or company something that conjures up images. When people can visualize your name with a picture, it's much easier for them to remember than an unfamiliar word or acronym that doesn't give their mind anything to latch on to. Think of an energy drink named Bloom. Now think of one named Enviga. Which name paints a picture? How's that for flower power?

One brand name loaded with visual imagery is Timberland, makers of rugged gear for the great outdoors. Whenever I hear that name, I imagine myself hiking in a mossy evergreen forest along a babbling brook, listening to lilting songbirds and crickets.

Even Dog Food Names Can Have Imagery

No matter what your product or company is, there is no excuse not to have a name with imagery. Pet food company Merrick recognizes the power of visually evocative names. Its canned dog food flavors conjure up some pretty tasty images: Thanksgiving Day Dinner, Grammy's Pot Pie, Cowboy Cookout, Smothered Comfort, Honolulu Luau. Merrick's names live up to their tagline, "It's food worthy of a fork." (For the record, I have not eaten any of these.)

Make Sure Your Name Has Imagery, Not Just Your Brand

Last week, someone wrote to me, "I've always liked the name Wells Fargo, because it connotes reliability and speed, and it has wonderful imagery of the Wild West. The stagecoach delivered the mail, come rain, snow, or ambush." Sure, after 162 years of building a successful brand and investing millions of dollars in advertising, the name Wells Fargo does evoke all of those things. But what if founders Henry Wells and William G. Fargo were starting a bank today and the name Wells Fargo popped up on your caller ID? What do those words alone conjure up without all of the years of visual branding? Certainly not pictures of the Wild West. Make sure your name has imagery from the beginning.

MORE EXAMPLES OF NAMES WITH IMAGERY

Range Rover (SUVs)	Irish Spring (soap)
Target (mass merchandiser)	Leap Frog (educational toys)
Hard Candy (nail polish)	

Legs —
Lends Itself to a Theme for Extended Mileage

To get the most out of your name, give it one that has legs. Strive for a theme with mileage you can build your brand around. Names with legs provide endless wordplay and verbal branding opportunities.

A strong theme can be extended to many elements of a brand, including these:

taglines	tradeshow themes
job titles	online promo codes
blog names	conference rooms
newsletter names	theme songs
network names	email signoffs
server names	company award names

Public relations pro, Lynette Hoy, is a fiery woman who isn't afraid to pick up the phone to pitch a great story about her clients to the press. When I met her, she was using her personal name as her business name: Lynette Hoy PR. Unfortunately, it didn't evoke anything about her high-energy personality or tenacity. So we branded her with a name and tagline that said it all: Firetalker PR. *Hot on the press.*

Lynette took it from there and ran with it, creating a firestorm of branding ideas. Her official title is Fire Chief. She works in The Firehouse. And her packages are called Inferno, Controlled Burn, and Matchbox. She lightly peppers her marketing materials with her theme, keeping it fresh and fun, but not cutesy, corny, or over the top. And the ringtone on her phone is the classic R&B funk song "Fire" by the Ohio Players, which she also cranks up during her speaking engagements to fire up the audience.

Find a Theme That Can Be Stretched like Carnival Taffy

Some especially rich themes with endless wordplay include *space exploration, nature, music, travel,* and *art.* The theme of food is also highly extendable, as we've discovered at Eat My Words:

✦ Blog name: *The Kitchen Sink*

✦ info@email: hungry@eatmywords.com

✦ Service packages: Snack, the Whole Enchilada, and Just the Meat

✦ Client parking sign: "Eat My Words' client parking only. Violators will be eaten."

✦ Business card: pink retro refrigerator (a replica of the one in our office, which we use as a bookcase)

✦ Wireless network name: Candyland

✦ Meeting materials: toast coasters, pens that look like licorice sticks, "Food for Thought" notepads

✦ Corporate workshops: Spilling the Beans

The Right Name Creates a Family

When you launch a product, you can't look into your crystal ball and know what the future holds. But developing a naming theme early on will help you tremendously down the road. Apple has done this well with the iMac, iPod, iPhone, iPad, and iTouch. And even though the word *cloud* has become terribly overused, the name iCloud is instantly identifiable as being from Apple, which makes it stand out from the rest of the cloud crowd. It works for them. (But it doesn't work for you or your products. Don't even go there.)

Republic of Tea has sub-brands with very long legs:

Get a Grip	Get Happy
Get Clean	Get Lost
Get Gorgeous	Get Smart

Trader Joe's has branded their ethnic foods with clever sub-brands that play off the primary name:

Trader Jose's (Mexican)	Trader Joe-San (Japanese)
Trader Ming's (Chinese)	Trader Jacque's (French)
Trader Giotto's (Italian)	

If your name doesn't have a theme, you can still extend it through the personality of the brand, as Ben & Jerry's has done:

Cherry Garcia	Chunky Monkey
Chocolate Therapy	Karamel Sutra
Chubby Hubby	Liz Lemon

Naming Product Versions

The easiest way to name product versions is with sequential numbers. Numbers help consumers quickly differentiate newer versus older. Numbering versions is especially appropriate in software because technology changes quickly. My current web browser is Firefox 24. While it's boring, it's clear.

On the other hand, Android is having fun by naming their versions after sweet indulgences: Cupcake, Donut, Eclair, Froyo, Gingerbread, Honeycomb, Ice Cream Sandwich, and Jelly Bean. Android's maker, Google, has also licensed the name KitKat from Nestlé in a clever promotional partnership. There are endless names Android can consider for future versions. Banana Split, Butterscotch, Cherry Pie, Lemon Bar, and Macaroon all sound good to me.

Another creative way to introduce new versions is with letters of the alphabet. Ford has done this by giving their models names that start with the letter "F":

Fairlane	Festiva
Fairmont	Futura
Falcon	Focus
Fiesta	Fusion

If you're going to try this, try using an initial letter that has many words associated with it, such as S, P, C, D, M, or A. Avoid limited letters such as K, Z, and X. (As a rule, it's never a good idea to start a name with the letter X, which makes pronunciation difficult. It's also the most difficult keystroke on a Qwerty keyboard.)

Names with Legs Can Mean Money

Despite the polarizing name, restaurant chain Hooters makes an obscene amount of money selling more than 250 types of merchandise featuring its name and silly slogans, including baby bibs that say "Show Me Your Hooters." Really.

If you have a catchy name that makes people smile, you can slap it on merchandise that people will pay for because they love your name and want to show it off. Think about that for a minute. You launch a new business without celebrity endorsements, brand recognition, or the cachet of Nike, Polo, or Louis Vuitton. Yet people are clamoring to buy and wear products with your name on it. Instead of you having to pay for advertising, your customers are paying you to advertise your brand. That is the true sign of a successful name. Here is some monetized merchandise we've created for food retailers.

Company	Monetized Merchandise
Church of Cupcakes	T-shirts that read "OMG" and "Forgive me Father, for I have binged."
Spoon Me (frozen yogurt)	T-shirts with the slogans "Shut-up and Spoon Me" and "If you love me, Spoon Me." Bumper stickers that read "If you're driving this close, you might as well Spoon Me."
Smitten (ice cream stores)	Branded T-shirts, totes, and infant bodysuits. "I'm Smitten" is on the back of the bodysuits, which looks adorable when the parent is holding the child.

Emotional —
Moves People

A recent *Fast Company* article revealed that 50 percent of every buying decision is driven by emotion. I'm not surprised. Think of how many times you have purchased a bottle of wine simply because the name made you smile. If you shop by the label as the majority of wine buyers do, it's hard to resist a love-at-first-sight name like Fat Bastard, 7 Deadly Zins, Layer Cake, Educated Guess, Little Black Dress, and Cat's Pee on a Gooseberry Bush. That's the power of a name that makes an emotional connection.

Use Emotion to Increase Sales

The hip Hotel Vitale on San Francisco's Embarcadero waterfront experienced a 25 percent jump in wedding business when we changed the ho-hum names of their wedding services to ones that were, pardon the pun, emotionally engaging.

Before	After
Rehearsal Dinner	Meet the Parents
Co-ed Bridal Shower	Shower Together
Post-Reception Bar Rental	Last Call for Alcohol
Post-Wedding Brunch	Bloody Married
Guest Rate	Entourage Rate

Previously, a bride and groom planning a wedding may have skimmed over a name like Post Reception Bar Rental, but nothing says party time like Last Call for Alcohol. That name makes an instant emotional connection because it's fun, meaningful, and loaded with imagery. And suddenly, a co-ed bridal shower doesn't sound so excruciating for the groom when it's named

Shower Together. All of these names bring levity to the stressful task of wedding planning, add value, and make everyone smile, even the parents footing the bill.

While I'd love to share more sales figures with you, name metrics cannot be quantified unless a name is changed. And even then, with refreshed branding and new advertising, the name cannot take all the credit. Hotel Vitale can attribute the 25 percent increase in wedding sales to the name changes because they were simply words listed in a guide. Nothing else changed. Restaurants can try this by changing the name of a dish on a menu. Something as simple as changing Chicken Soup to the more emotionally driven Grandma's Chicken Soup will increase sales.

The Power of Love

Speaking of happily ever after, we all know that falling in love is a powerful emotion. When Eat My Words was charged with naming a new online dating website, we wanted the name to tap into those feelings. The company who hired us was eHarmony. While I loved the people we worked with there, I cringed at the name eHarmony, which is dated and pretty cheesy. Most dating websites have dreadful names. Who really wants to say they met the love of their life on eHarmony, Christian Mingle, Farmers Only, Fuzd, or Veggie Dates?

The new website eHarmony had created was for people who wanted a relationship but weren't necessarily ready to get "Bloody Married." We explored the positive emotions of romance and seized on the feelings people get when they are super excited about meeting someone new who they really, really like. You probably know that rush of excitement and happiness. It's the best feeling in the world. We landed on *Jazzed*, a timeless word that people in the target audience are comfortable saying. It's not only an emotional name, it's literally an emotion. And a nice little bonus was that, like eHarmony, *Jazzed* evokes music. The client loved the name and launched the site.

Like most online dating relationships, Jazzed.com didn't last as long as we had hoped. (They couldn't match the success of

Match.com and eHarmony didn't want to cannibalize its own business.) I'm still heartbroken.

MORE EXAMPLES OF EMOTIONAL NAMES

Obsession (fragrance)

Pedigree (pet food)

Club Monaco (clothing)

Snuggle (fabric softener)

One Kings Lane (flash sale site)

Next let's look at the flipside of SMILE: SCRATCH.

CHAPTER 2

The 7 Deadly Sins

When you're starting out with a blank slate, don't curse your name with *any* disadvantages. Every time you have to help people spell, pronounce, and understand your name, you are essentially apologizing for it, which devalues your brand.

Unique spellings, nonsensical words, and unfamiliar expressions may differentiate you, but just because it's different doesn't mean it's good. There's a terribly misguided belief that *unique* equals *creative*, which equals *great*. Think of a time when you've been in an art gallery, at a garage sale, or in the home of a friend, and you eyed a strange oil painting, turned to the person next to you, and whispered, "What were they smoking?" People react the same way to strange names.

For a glimpse at the seriously strange, you need to look no

further than the annual winners of TechCrunch Disrupt, a breeding ground of awesome startups with not-so-awesome names. Past winners include Atmosphir, Bojam, GazoPa, plaYce, Shwowp, Tollim, and Tweegee. Distinctive names? Yes. Good names? Hardly.

When to SCRATCH It Off the List

As you know from the previous chapter, the SMILE & SCRATCH name evaluation test is based on my philosophy, "A name should make you smile instead of scratch your head." We've covered SMILE, the acronym for the five qualities of a great name. SCRATCH is an acronym for the seven deal breakers. A good way to remember this: if it makes you scratch your head, scratch it off the list.

SCRATCH: The 7 Deadly Sins

Spelling challenged

Copycat

Restrictive

Annoying

Tame

Curse of Knowledge

Hard to pronounce

If you want a strong name, make sure it doesn't suffer from any of these weaknesses.

Spelling Challenged —
Not Spelled like It Sounds

If you have to spell your name out loud for people, Siri butchers it, or it looks like a typo, it's a mistake.

Spelling your brand name in a non-intuitive way isn't clever—it's lazy. Sure, it's tempting to spell your name creatively, so you can nab an available domain name. But spelling-challenged names will forever frustrate your customers, embarrass your employees, and annoy journalists, bloggers, and proofreaders. And if you were still in elementary school, it would annoy your teacher, too. (Many dot-com names do look like second graders created them. More about those dot-com name fails in Chapter 3.)

Misspelled Hell

For many years, my firm has bestowed a "Head Scratcher of the Year" prize to companies with extremely problematic names. The 2010 winner was ridiculously silly: an organic baby clothing company named (drum roll, please) Speesees.

Obviously, whoever came up with this name was not a former spelling bee champion. I've been in the naming business long enough to bet money on why they spelled it that way—the domain name they wanted (Species.com) wasn't available, so they thought they would be clever by spelling the word phonetically.

On its Facebook page, Speesees explains that it's "spelled s-p-e-e-s-e-e-s because that's the way a baby might spell 'species' (if a baby could spell)." I am not making this up.

Imagine that you work in sales at Speesees.com. Making sales calls, you have to repeat your email address (e.g., staceyw@speesees.com) over the phone. Ten times a day. This is what you would sound like: "That's Stacey with an *e*—S-T-A-C-E-Y-W—at Speesees dot com. S-P-E-E-S-E-E-S. I know it's a weird spelling, but we think that's how babies might spell it if babies could spell." Having to say this *once* would be exasperating. But how many times in the life of your business will you have to spell your email address or URL for someone? Why would you intentionally make it hard for yourself with a spelling-challenged name?

Beyond the babyish spelling, Speesees is a creepy name for anything related to human babies. Plus, Speesees broke what I thought was a self-evident, unwritten rule of naming, which I will write here, so you don't make the same mistake—your business name should not rhyme with *feces*.

Speesees is now out of business. The last image on their Facebook page is for a "bye-bye sale." Bye-bye, baby.

Don't Get Cute with Numbers

While it may work for texting and clever license plates, embedding numbers in a brand name looks cutesy and unprofessional. When you use numbers in your name you will 4ever have 2 spell it out. For example, coast2coast spelled out loud would be coast-*numeral* 2-coast. Your goal is to have a name that you can say proudly: "Coast to Coast dot com—just like it sounds." If you can't get the domain name CoastToCoast.com, add a modifier word (as in GoCoastToCoast.com or FlyCoastToCoast.com.)

Skimming through store names at Mall of America (a hotbed of bad names), I found stores called Friends 2b Made and Engrave Ur Memory. Friends, I would like to engrave this into your memory: if it's not spelled the way it sounds, scratch it off the list.

Test the Siri Theory

The true test to see if a name is spelling challenged is to see and hear how voice recognition software spells it. Use the microphone key on an iPhone and speak the name as a text message. See how it's spelled. Is it incorrect? Garbled? Did autocorrect suggest an absurdly wrong word, as every spell-check program will forever do to you and your customers? Welcome to your world.

While you have an iPhone handy, use voice commands to ask Siri to do a Google search for the brand name you're considering. Whatever results you get are what your customers will see.

MORE EXAMPLES OF SPELLING-CHALLENGED NAMES:

TCHO (fancy chocolate)   Houzz (interior design)

Svbtle (publishing network)   Häagen-Dazs (ice cream)

Twyxt (couples app)

I'd like to buy a vowel, please.

Copycat —
Similar to a Competitor

Hijacking another company's original idea isn't good for your business reputation or for building trust with your customers. Copycat names are lazy, lack originality, and blatantly ride on a competitor's coattails. Plus, because they could cause customer confusion, you open yourself up to trademark infringement, which can be very costly.

Pinkberry is a successful chain of trendy frozen yogurt stores. While the name isn't exactly a showstopper, because of the popularity of the brand, countless copycats have tried to take a free ride on the highly distinctive Pinkberry name and unique swirl identity design. Here are a handful of the dozens of knockoff names I've come across. A number of these have faced trademark infringement and related claims. (See the Resources section for more on trademarking your name.)

Yoberry	Lemonberry
Peachberry	Blissberry
Yogiberry	Myberry
Kiwiberry	Luvberry
Coolberry	Freshberry

Another example of a copycatted name is Twitter, a polarizing name that I love. I think we can all agree that the employee collaboration tools named Yammer, Jabber, and Chatter were inspired by the name Twitter. While those three names may not be cause for trademark infringement, they are not winning any awards for originality. I got a good laugh when we recently worked on naming a cool new corporate employee communication platform. In the creative brief under "Words to Avoid," our client wrote, "Any sound a bird makes." (I was thrilled that he chose the name Tribewire.)

Other Copycat Trends to Avoid:

+ ____ Monkey
+ ____ Rocket
+ ____ Daddy
+ ____.ly (.ly domain names, especially verbs, look and sound sil.ly)
+ iAnything (unless you're Apple, don't do this—it screams copycat)
+ eAnything (e.g., eFax and eLove are hopelessly dated, plus they look grammatically incorrect in print as proper nouns)
+ uAnything (see eAnything)
+ The Double-O (it may have worked for Google and Yahoo, but that doesn't guarantee the success of Doostang)
+ any fruit (Apple and Blackberry are so well known that if you name your company Kumquat, you will be a copycat *and* you'll have a silly name)
+ Cloud (overused, and because most businesses now have an Internet presence in the cloud, the word *cloud* is superfluous)

Also avoid names that are a combination of a random color plus a noun. While it works for some companies, where the color is meaningful to their audience, such as WhiteHat Security ("white hats" are the good guys), most names with colors in them, especially those of tech companies and wine brands, sound terribly dated.

An Exception to the Copycat Rule

While it would be ideal to have a unique brand name that no one else has ever used before, with only twenty-six letters in the English alphabet, that's nearly impossible to do. Especially if you want people to be able to spell and pronounce your name. The good news is, it's usually not a problem for unrelated brands to have the same name when your audience is not likely to be confused about who is who. When a name appears in context on a product, people don't associate it with the other brand. Think about it. When you're showering with Dove soap, you don't associate it with a chocolate-covered Dove Bar.

Here are some other examples of unrelated brands that share the same name:

Monster (job board, energy drink, cable company)

Ritz (crackers, hotel)

Explorer (car, Internet browser)

Pandora (Internet radio, jewelry)

Delta (airline, faucets)

Magnum (condoms, ice cream)

I don't recommend using the same name as a brand that's so recognizable it's iconic. For instance, using either *Apple* or *Virgin* would be a liability for you and almost certainly run into issues of trademark infringement. Always check with a trademark attorney before using any name.

Restrictive —
Locks You In, Limits Growth

On average, Americans visit tire shops only a handful of times in their lives. Yet in Canada, according to *Reference for Business*, nine out of ten adults shop once a week at Canadian Tire. It's not that the roads up north are so rough that people need to replace their wheels fifty-two times a year. Canadian Tire sells not only tires, but toasters, treadmills, tackle boxes, tool belts, trashcans, tents, tablecloths, toys, tropical plants, telescopes, and trampolines. And a whole lot of other totally terrific merchandise completely unrelated to tires. Like the company's tagline said in the 80s, "There is a lot more to Canadian Tire than tires." What a waste of words. A tagline shouldn't have to apologize for your name.

With 437 locations in Canada, it's safe to say that the Canucks know Canadian Tire is a mass merchandiser. But what if Canadian Tire wanted to roll into the United States with the same name? How would Americans know that they could go there to buy everything from toilet seats to tennis balls? Hello, million-dollar ad campaign.

Don't get locked into a name that you may outgrow down the road. Plan ahead, and choose a name that will be a wide enough umbrella to cover your future product and service offerings.

Do Not Use the Same Name for Your Product and Company

It's confusing and shortsighted to name your product and company the same thing. Although you may have only one product now, think about the future. What if Apple had named their first computer the Apple? What would they name the dozens of other products that have launched since then? Your company name should allow any product name under it.

If you're launching a product and company simultaneously, I suggest you name your product first. You can expect consumers to remember only one name, so make it what they're actually buying.

Don't Paint Yourself into a Corner

Roomba, the first robotic vacuum, was the initial product from iRobot. The folks in the marketing department probably thought they were onto something clever when they named their second product, a wet vac, Scooba. Then they were stuck. They ran out of -ba names. How do their next two robots—Verro (for pools) and Looj (for gutters)—fit in? They don't.

Name	Limiting Factor
99¢ Only Stores	It outgrew the price.
Fast Signs	Its tagline is "More than fast. More than signs."
24-Hour Fitness	Some locations are not open 24 hours.
Burlington Coat Factory	They now sell many kinds of clothing and home furnishings and have spent millions explaining their name: "We're more than just coats. Not affiliated with Burlington Industries."
Diapers.com	They sell all kinds of baby products, not just diapers.
1-800-FLOWERS	This has got to be the least romantic name ever for a company that now sells not only flowers but candy, fruit, gift baskets, teddy bears, and more.

Annoying —
Forced, Frustrates Customers

Annoying of course is subjective, but if you think about your name from a customer's point of view, you can avoid causing frustration if your name does not appear forced, random, or grammatically incorrect.

Clunky Coined Names

If you invent a new word for your name, be careful that it doesn't sound unnatural. Mashing two words together or mixing up a bunch of letters to form a new word rarely appears or sounds smooth. One of the most cringe-worthy coined names I've come across is a women's networking organization named Femfessionals. Really? Would you want that on a professional résumé?

Some natural and organic brands that use this technique end up with names that sound like they are full of chemicals (e.g., Activia and Enviga). Simply adding or dropping a vowel or two at the end of a real word or word root is the laziest way to coin a name and almost always sounds forced (e.g., Innova, Natura, Portfolia, and Evolva.) Exceptions would be Nautica and Expedia. Those are pretty names, which sound like real words and are no-brainers to spell.

Another naming style that tries too hard is adding trendy suffixes to a word to make up a new word. Sprayology, Teaosophy, and Perfumania are all train wrecks. Also, please don't dissect the word *Nirvana*. It's a beautiful word on its own but rarely works when combined with another word. Homevana, Teavana, and Pervana are all uncomfortably forced.

Suffixes that need to be used with caution:

____-mania	____-ster
____-osophy	____-icious
____-ology	____-zilla
____-palooza	____-ly
____-topia	____-ella

Resist the Temptation to Be Mysterious

Another sure-fire way to annoy people is to choose a name that's completely random and seemingly meaningless. One I wonder about a lot is Vungle. I have no idea what this company does. I don't want to know. It sounds like an STD. Likewise, can you guess what companies Qdoba, Magoosh, Iggli, Kiip, Zippil, or Zumper do?

Don't Get Thrown in the Grammar Slammer

A grammatically challenged name is unprofessional, a huge turnoff to customers, and sets a bad example for children. A few of these names that should receive citations from the grammar police are Ruth's Chris Steakhouse, Retail Me Not, Jennifer Convertibles, and Toys "R" Us, which in seven short letters manages to violate at least three basic rules of English.

Initials Don't Make Good Names

Nancy Andreotta and Colleen Kachele are professional organizers who market a nifty reusable labeling system for home storage. The name they created for their business, NACKit!, combined their initials, NA and CK, which was meaningful to them but annoying to potential customers. NACKit! was also spelling challenged, had an unnecessary exclamation point, and an awkward combination of upper and lowercase letters.

When Nancy and Colleen received a trademark infringement letter from 3M brand (makers of Post-it Notes and Post-it Products), they had to agree to change their name to avoid litigation. We rebranded NACKit! as Stash Mob, a fun name that hints at storing your stuff, is easy for people to spell, and doesn't slow down Siri or spell check.

Tame —
Flat, Descriptive, Uninspired

If you want your name to stand out in a sea of sameness and get noticed—without a massive advertising budget—you can't afford to be shy. Descriptive names are boring because they require so little imagination. They don't challenge, excite, or mentally stimulate us. And because they are so predictable, chances are that those names have already been taken, making it difficult to get them trademarked.

While descriptive names say exactly what your product or company is, they reveal nothing about the personality of your brand (other than exposing your lack of creativity). And when you draw from a limited pool of descriptive words, you sound like everyone else, making your name indistinguishable from competitors. Nowhere is this more relevant today than cloud services. Here are a handful of some of the hundreds of names in the cloud crowd.

Cloud2b	Cloud Bus	Cloud Pad
Cloud 2.0	Cloud Net	Cloud Set
Cloud 365	Cloud Now	Cloud Tek
Cloud 9	Cloud One	Cloud Web

Other than Cloud 9, which is easy to remember because it's a familiar phrase, the above names fall flat because they don't stand out in a sea of sameness. The word *cloud* has become so overused that San Francisco's techie hivemind is trying to brand their mid-Market neighborhood as *Cloud Corridor*. Apparently human resource directors are very excited about this. *SFist* reported, "If *Cloud Corridor* sounds insufferable, it's because the *The Cloud* is just a trendy marketing term to begin with— one that has suddenly become so ubiquitous it hardly means anything." I wish locals would just go back to calling the area Twittertown. I seriously love that name.

When Descriptive Names Make Sense

If your customers are trying to find information quickly, and you are offering multiple choices, descriptive names can be very helpful, such as FedEx Priority Overnight, FedEx International Next Flight and FedEx Ground.

MORE EXAMPLES OF TAME NAMES

DocuSign (electronic signatures)

AcuPOLL (research)

Enfagrow (toddler formula)

Network Solutions (domain names)

Kmart (mass merchandiser)

Curse of Knowledge —
Only Insiders Get It

No one is more of an expert on the company or product you are naming than you. But when communicating with potential customers who are unfamiliar with your world, insider knowledge can become a curse. We can't unlearn what we know, so we find it extremely difficult to think like a newbie. We talk in acronyms, internal shorthand, code words, and industry jargon—all of which sounds like a foreign language to outsiders. Don't alienate potential customers.

According to Wikipedia, the curse of knowledge is described as "a cognitive bias to which better-informed people find it extremely difficult to think about problems from the perspective of lesser-informed people." This essentially means that when we know something, it becomes hard for us to imagine not knowing it. As a result, we become bad communicators of our own ideas. Coined by TV music composer Robin Hogarth, the term *curse of knowledge* got on my radar thanks to my favorite business book, *New York Times* bestseller *Made to Stick: Why Some Ideas Survive and Others Die*, by Dan and Chip Heath. Just as ideas with the curse of knowledge aren't sticky, neither are names.

If you have a television and don't fast-forward through the commercials, chances are you've seen an ad for the pain relief patch Salonpas. The first time I heard it, I thought *Salonpas* was an unattractive amalgamation of two pretty French words, *salon* and *pas*. That didn't make much sense to me, but I couldn't imagine what else it could mean. According to the Salonpas website, the name is derived from its active ingredient, methyl salicylate. It goes on to explain: "Methyl Salicylate passes through the skin and goes directly to the site of your pain, right where it hurts. Therefore, Salonpas represents *Salicylate + Pass*." Seriously? I need a Salonpas for my brain.

Avoid Alphanumeric Brain-benders

Jumbled words and letters, especially in consumer electronics, may signify something to the employees at Best Buy, but for shoppers, they are annoying and meaningless. A few years back, Eat My Words renamed some products for consumer audio company Altec Lansing. While I don't remember the alphabet soup of all of the original names, these are pretty close: M202, HX8020, VS63. Any idea what those are? What type of emotional connection are you feeling? They make my head hurt. Here's the before and after transformation:

Altec Lansing Product	Original Alpha-numeric Name	New Consumer-Friendly Name
iPod docking station for the bedroom	M202	Moondance
Sleek in-home speakers	HX8020	Expressionist
Hipster headphones	VS63	Backbeat

Make Sure Your Name Is Not Cursed in a Foreign Language

Of all of the anxieties people have about their new name, "What if it means something dirty in a foreign language?" has the highest fear factor and the lowest chance of actually happening. That legendary story you learned in business school about the Chevy Nova selling poorly in Spanish-speaking countries because its name translated as "doesn't go"? Total bunk. The myth is clearly dispelled at Snopes.com.

Mistakes occasionally happen, such as when Colgate introduced toothpaste in France named Cue, the same name as a notorious French porn magazine.

If you are planning on having a global brand, I do recommend you have a professional linguistic study done by a firm that specializes in this (not just your friend who speaks French). You can find some of these companies listed in the Resources section.

MORE EXAMPLES OF NAMES WITH THE CURSE OF KNOWLEDGE

Name	Meaning
Starbucks "Tall" (small coffee size)	When Starbucks started, *Tall* was a large. Now it's considered a *small*.
Eukanuba (pet food)	During the Jazz Era, it meant "the tops" or "something supreme."
Mzinga (social software)	From *mzinga*, Zulu for "ring" and the Swahili word for "beehive"
SPQR (San Francisco restaurant)	Latin for "The Senate and the Roman People"
Umpqua (national bank)	River in Oregon

Is Your Name in *Urban Dictionary*?

If your brand is targeted at teens or young adults, be sure to look up your name in *Urban Dictionary* (urbandictionary.com) before you give it the green light. While at one time a fun place to poke around, *Urban Dictionary* appears to have been taken over by hormonal teenage boys and is now a hotbed of more than seven million definitions of street slang words and phrases, most of them sexually explicit, homophobic, misogynistic, moronic, and intentionally disgusting. It has killed many great names for our clients, including Pearl Diver and Saltminer. (I'll let you look up the definitions.)

Don't panic if there is one untoward definition with a few

thumbs-up votes from users of the site. But if your name has a lot of unfortunate definitions and more than a handful of thumbs-up votes, you may want to reconsider as it's likely already part of the teen lexicon (or *sexicon*, so to speak).

Hard to Pronounce —
Not Obvious, Unapproachable

After more than twenty years and just as many shameful attempts, I have finally mastered the pronunciation of one of my favorite French dishes, *Salad Niçoise*. When I recently ordered it in front of my new client, I was thrilled that I didn't embarrass myself. Lunch was *très magnifique*. Then I saw the dessert menu. The object of my desire was described as "delicate layers of flakey golden puff pastry, whipped cream, and homemade strawberry jam, dusted with confectioner's sugar." It was called a *mille-feuille*. I didn't have a clue how to say it. The other choices, clafoutis, *kouign amann*, and "La Côte Basque's Dacquoise," were equally intimidating. I ordered a cup of decaf and a slice of humble pie.

I imagine a lot of us have encountered a similar situation stumbling over the pronunciation of foreign food. Equally challenging are European fashion brands such as Hermès, Louis Vuitton, and Givenchy. Recently I was at a Bulgari jewelry exhibit and was mortified when I pronounced it "BULL gary" in front of my two friends who corrected me and simultaneously said, "BULL guh ree." Of course, these names are fine because they are easy to pronounce in their countries of origin. But haute couture aside, many names derived from foreign languages are unapproachable simply because most Americans (myself included) don't know how to pronounce them and don't want to make fools of themselves trying.

Also problematic are made-up names that are not intuitive to pronounce. I recently saw a catering service with an unappetizing name: Chewes. I had no idea if it's pronounced "chews," or "chewies." I instructed Siri, "Find chews catering." She replied,

"I found fifteen *shoe* stores. Eleven of them are close to you."
She also couldn't find "chewies catering," but instead gave me
Chili Lemon Garlic restaurant, which sounded delicious. I made
a reservation and still don't know how to pronounce Chewes.

Capital Punishment

Do not spell or design your name with all capital letters because
people will be confused by the pronunciation. Here are a
few examples:

Name	Pronunciation Problem
OPI (nail polish)	Mistakenly pronounced "O pee," like Opie, the kid from *The Andy Griffith Show*
SAP (software)	Can be pronounced "sap," as in "sad and pathetic." Employees of SAP's chief competitor, Oracle, love using the "sap" pronunciation, dripping with sarcastic ooze.
THX (audio company)	Mistakenly pronounced "thanks," because it looks like the common abbreviation for that word.
TCBY (frozen yogurt)	Doesn't roll off the tongue, and it's just as annoying as the chest-pounding name it stands for: "The Country's Best Yogurt"
TCHO (gourmet chocolate)	The uppercase letters of this name on their packaging make it look like an acronym, but it's just a word no one can pronounce. Is it supposed to be short for "Techno" or is the "T" silent? Or is it the sound people make when they sneeze? We'll never Tknow.

Avoid Acronyms

Speaking of capital letters, FYI, people have ADD. You can expect them to remember only one name, not two. Brand your product with a name (e.g., World of Warcraft) and let the acronym (WOW) be something you use internally.

Corporations are notorious for having endless acronyms. Cathy Bennett, Chief Launch Officer of Start The Startup, told me a funny story: "While I was at Ford Motor Company, some executives decided we had too many acronyms. They set up a team to compile a reference book for employees. Quite logically, they named the team the Ford Acronym Review Team, aka FART."

Two Pronunciations Is Double Trouble

Words that can be pronounced two different ways are also pronunciation pitfalls. With the proliferation of eco-friendly products and companies that have sprouted up in the last ten years, the prefix *eco-* has been terribly overused. Unfortunately, *eco-* rarely works in a name because there are two ways to pronounce it—"ee-co" and "echo"—which can cause consumer confusion and weaken the brand. For instance, is the name Ecover pronounced "EE cover," "ECK over," or "ee KO ver"? Don't make your customers guess. No one wants to say it wrong and be embarrassed. There are exceptions—food company Alter Eco (a play on *alter ego*), is clearly pronounced as "Alter EE co," as opposed to "Alter ECK o," since we know it rhymes with *ego*.

Punctuation Is a Crutch

Lastly, if your name needs the visual crutch of punctuation (güd), or a lowercase first letter (uSamp) to aid in pronunciation, it's not a good name. Also, you can't rely on letters in different colors to show people how to pronounce it. Your name will not appear in color in the press or in search engine results. Your name needs to be able to appear in black and white as a proper noun in the *Wall Street Journal*.

Backward Is the Wrong Way to Go

Like Xobni, most names spelled backward are unpronounce-able. Tennis superstar Serena Williams's clothing line is named Aneres. How do you say that? A backward name that *does* work well is Harpo, the name of Oprah Winfrey's production company. It sounds like a real word, has memorable imagery (Harpo Marx), and makes us smile in either direction it's written.

MORE EXAMPLES OF NAMES THAT ARE HARD TO PRONOUNCE

Name	Incorrect Pronunciation	Correct Pronunciation
Giro (bike gear)	as if it rhymed with *hero*	As in *gyroscope*
Fage (yogurt)	Fahj, or as if it rhymed with *page*	FAH yay
Saucony (running shoes & apparel)	saw KOHnee, or SAUCE uh nee	Sock uh nee
Sur La Table (kitchenware)	Sir lah TAY bull	Sir lah TAHB (Don't say "TAH bleu" unless you are French.)
Pardot (marketing automation)	Par DOUGH, as if it were French	PAR dot

CHAPTER 3

Strategies, Secrets, and Silliness

The desperation to find an available domain name has gotten so extreme that a grammar-checking and proofreading company is calling itself Grammarly. Even more cringe-worthy is its ridiculous domain name: www.grammar.ly. In case you missed the memo, -.ly is the country-specific domain extension for Libya. Serious.ly. I've been to Libya and even I didn't know that.

Using common sense rather than blindly following trends, especially those started by fashion-challenged engineers, is critical when it comes to domain names, also known as URLs. (To refresh your memory, URL is the abbreviation for universal resource locator. This is another example of what happens when engineers are allowed to name things.)

It Didn't Stop Facebook . . .

Many successful online businesses, including Dropbox (get dropbox.com), Square (squareup.com), Basecamp (basecamp hq.com), Box (box.net), and SlideShare (slideshare.net), started off with an imperfect domain name before hitting it big. They then spent undisclosed sums to purchase the exact match domain. Facebook, which started out as thefacebook.com, reportedly paid $200,000 in 1995 for facebook.com. SlideShare and Square continue to use their original domain names as their official URL. Ironically, Flickr, whom I curse for starting the looks-like-a-typo trend, eventually broke down and purchased flicker.com.

Google Eliminates the Problem

Think about what you do when you accidentally type the wrong URL into your web browser. For instance, if you want to go to the website for Delta Faucets, you type in "delta.com." But you accidentally end up at Delta Airlines. Whoa! What do you do? Book a plane ticket to Poughkeepsie? Have a meltdown because Delta Faucets doesn't own delta.com? Refuse to do business with them because they greatly inconvenienced you? No. You simply search for "Delta Faucets," and instantly find them. And you probably don't even notice what their domain name is. You don't care. No one does.

Put Yourself Out of Your Misery

Most people believe that the first thing they must do when naming a business is to go to a domain registrar (e.g., GoDaddy) to make sure the domain name isn't taken. And if an exact match isn't available (and they don't have thousands of dollars to buy one that's parked), they think they have to dismiss the name entirely. Countless great names have been killed that way. Worse, countless bad names have been conceived for the same reason. I know that many terrible names are the result of the URL being available for $9.95. (Note: I use the amount of $9.95 throughout the book as an average price of any available domain.) Here are some likely suspects:

Squrl	Kyte	Shyp
Birst	Scanja	Fiverr
Takkle	Gliffy	Kwiry
Ipiit	SmolkSignal	Oqo
Piczo	Innotas	iShryk
Mogad	Zippii	Qunify
Loud3r	Inboxq	Clixter

3 Strategies to Get a Good Domain Name for $9.95

Here are three simple strategies that will help you nab a domain name that people can spell, pronounce, and understand.

Strategy #1: Add Another Word or Two

Bliss, the wildly popular brand of skin care and spas, couldn't get Bliss.com, which is in use by Glam Media, so they got Bliss-World.com. Pure happiness.

If you're a scrappy startup, self-funded, or simply don't want to fork over big bucks for a domain, a second word is the way to go. Adding a modifier to your name in the form of an extra word or two is now a common and perfectly acceptable way to get an available domain name and help your customers find you through search engines.

Imagine that you have come up with a clever name for your new candle company: Fireworks. You are devastated to see that a fireworks company is using www.sells.Fireworks.com. Do not extinguish your brand name! If someone trying to find you ends up at Fireworks.com by mistake they will not give up. It takes seconds to go to Google, type in "Fireworks candles," and find your website.

What about people too lazy to go to Google, you ask? People looking for candles don't randomly type "Fireworks" into their web browser. (Just as people looking for naming services don't randomly type in EatMyWords.com.)

If you want strangers to find you on Google, make sure your website is rich in real content (as opposed to unnaturally cluttered with keywords), so you are attractive to search engines. A good copywriter, SEO (search engine optimization) pro, or SEM (Search Engine Marketing) expert can be of tremendous value here.

The customers who want to do business with you already know your name. Maybe they read about your candles in a magazine, enjoyed them in the home of a friend, or saw them in a shop while on vacation and didn't want to lug them back on the plane to Poughkeepsie.

In this case, an obvious domain name to get would be Fire worksCandles.com. Not only does adding a descriptive word reinforce what your business is, the descriptive modifier will help search engines find you.

What if FireworksCandles.com is parked by someone who is selling it for $5000? Unless you have money to burn, don't do it! Just try some different words with it, such as FireworksShop.com, FireworksStore.com, or BuyFireworks.com. Those domain names don't sound like company names, and no one will think your business is named Buy Fireworks. But they will know how to find you online.

To turn your domain name into a call to action, try using a verb in front of your name (e.g., EnjoyCoke.com, GetDropbox.com, or GoIncase.com). Here are some verbs and short words you can use to help find an available domain name:

Buy ____	My ____	____ Co
Drink ____	The ____	____ Global
Drive ____	Try ____	____ Group
Eat ____	Shop ____	____ Inc
Enjoy ____	WeAre ____	____ Online
Get ____	Your ____	____ Store
Go ____	____ App	____ Tech

Strategy #2: Use a Creative Phrase

A creative phrase as a domain name can reinforce your brand, aid in SEO, and make people smile.

When I named a frozen yogurt store Rehab, the client got the domain name, GetMeToRehab.com. Not only is it a fun call to action, teens love to say it, and the URL doesn't clutter up the T-shirts—it makes people want to wear them.

As demonstrated with the candle store, it's easy to find an available URL simply by adding a word to your name. While that's perfectly acceptable, a more creative technique would be to use a catchy phrase instead. In the case of Fireworks candles, I would suggest one with a little romantic spark. For instance:

FireworksInTheBedroom.com

FireworksHappen.com

ISmellFireworks.com

LightMyFireworks.com

Again, these domain names will not be confused with your company name. They will make people smile, reinforce your brand, and make your URL super sticky.

Speaking of unforgettable URLs, every January I attend the Fancy Food Show in San Francisco. For two and a half days, I meander up and down the aisles, grazing on cookies, chocolate, crackers, candy, cheese, and countless carbs and calories. While the dizzying displays of deliciousness are certainly memorable, most of the names are not. But I will never forget what I saw in 2012, emblazoned on a banner at the Peanut Butter & Co. booth:

www.ILovePeanutButter.com

That sign stopped me in my tracks. I loved it so much I took a picture. But I didn't need to. ILovePeanutButter.com is forever etched in my brain. That's the power of using a catchy phrase for your domain name. Again, Peanut Butter & Co. is the company name. And they have that domain name, peanutbutterandco .com, too. But which is easier and more fun for them to say when they tell people their website and email addresses? Which is more of a conversation starter on their business cards? Which is easier for people to remember? Which one makes people smile? Clearly the company knows, because if you type www.Peanut ButterAndCo.com into your browser, it automatically redirects to www.ILovePeanutButter.com.

Strategy #3: Get a .net or .biz Extension

While a .com extension is the most desirable one for business, don't automatically rule out alternate extensions such as .net or .biz. Just as we ran out of 800 numbers and transitioned to 888, 877, and 866 without batting an eye, no one will think your business is untrustworthy if you have a .biz or .net name.

When I started Eat My Words nearly ten years ago, the .com domain wasn't available, so I bought EatMyWords.biz. I had hundreds of expensive business cards printed with the .biz URL. (I put the .biz part of the URL in hot pink ink to make it pop.) Six weeks later, EatMyWords.com became available. I snatched it up for $1200, but I kept the old business cards and still use them without apology. No one has ever commented on it.

5 Domain Name Secrets

Here are some secrets I've learned after years of dreaming up domain names for my clients.

Secret #1: Not All Names Are Taken

My clients have secured these exact match domain names and many others for $9.95:

BreedTrust.com (pet services review site)

BoldMatters.com (personal development)

RickshawRepublic.com (restaurant)

IHaveABean.com (specialty grade coffee)

GardenConfetti.com (microgreen shakers)

Secret #2: Make a Lowball Offer

If your dream domain name is parked or listed for sale, it doesn't hurt to inquire about the price and make a lower offer. Our urban storage client, Boxbee, negotiated its domain for a few hundred bucks.

Secret #3: Buy the Misspellings

If you have a word in your name that people often misspell (e.g., mortgage, vacuum, library), in addition to the correct spelling of your domain, buy common misspellings of it. You can simply have those incorrect URLs automatically redirected it to the correct one. That way, people will get to your website even if they misspell your URL. And they will be none the wiser. Really.

Secret #4: URLs Don't Need Keywords

Google no longer favors keyword-rich domain names (e.g., best-spas.com, cheapinkcartridges.com, travelbargains.com). These kinds of names are very hard to trademark because as descriptive phrases they don't identify the source of the goods or services. If a catchy brand name or domain name has the right SEO, contains relevant content-rich text, and is lightly peppered with targeted keywords that blend into your copy naturally, it can easily top Google results. Content should be written for customers first and search engines second. For best results, hire an SEO expert and a crafty copywriter.

Secret #5: Longer Names Are OK

The popular belief is that a short domain name is better than a long one because it will be easier to remember. That's not always true. According to a recent article in *Forbes*, DollarShaveClub. com has net sales of around $1.1 million each month. And how can anyone forget the fabulous name of the online furnishings store PreviouslyOwnedByAGayMan.com?

If a longer name is more descriptive and easier to comprehend, it will be more memorable than a short, meaningless name. For example, rcbn.com is short but completely meaningless. It won't mean anything to potential customers or a search engine because there are no real words in it. However, if that is an acronym for a business named Rapid City Book Nook, then RapidCityBookNook.com would have meaning for human eyes and search engines. So short isn't always better.

Short names became popular for .coms, giving everyone the false impression that a short domain name was essential. While it may have been good to have a short name years ago, now it's not important because web browsers magically auto-fill addresses while we type them. And what good is a short name if it's completely meaningless, hard to spell, and impossible to pronounce?

A recent check of a secondary domain name seller revealed many four- and five-letter domain names for sale. How many can you pronounce? How many would be spelled correctly with voice recognition software?

Aacax	Jouee	Teliq
Akke	Joxly	Tuova
Azrio	Kryse	Umiro
Bhib	Oivo	Vius
Calq	Ooay	Xaca
Duqa	Paxxt	Ziavo
Exoot	Takaj	Mozid

All of the above empty-vessel names are listed for sale for thousands of dollars. Whoever buys them will have to spend even more money making them actually mean something.

5 Silly Ideas to Steer Clear Of

Here are some amateur mistakes to watch out for.

Silly Idea #1: Spell It Creatively

While I covered this in SCRATCH, I must drill this into your head because it's by far the biggest mistake people make when naming their company. The problem with having a brand name like Naymz, Takkle, Flickr, or Speesees is that you will forever have to spell it when you say it because it isn't spelled how people hear it. And voice recognition software won't understand it either.

If you and your employees have to spell your name out loud for people, you are wasting everyone's time and apologizing for it over and over and over again. Resist the temptation of getting one of these domains just because it's available for $9.95.

Sil.ly Idea #2: Use an Obscure Domain Extension to Spell Your Name

While it's tempting to create a domain name using a country code Top Level Domain (ccTLD) extension such as .me for Montenegro, .it for Italy, .us for United States, and .io for Indian Ocean Territory, those names are tru.ly troubleso.me. In addition to being difficult to spell, ccTLD domain names can be hard to pronounce, especially when unaided by a visual identity. How do you pronounce Copio.us? Is it "Copio dot U S" or "Copious"? Equally troublesome is that the human eye is trained to stop when it reads a period. So a name like Copio.us causes people to stop reading. For all the wrong reasons.

A few years ago, rather quietly, the social bookmarking web service del.icio.us renamed itself Delicious because the domain name was so problematic to spell. The company explained the name change this way: "We've seen a zillion different confusions and misspellings of 'del.icio.us' over the years (for example, 'de.licio.us', 'del.icio.us.com', and 'del.licio.us'), so moving to delicious.com will make it easier for people to find the site and share it with their friends."

One final word of caution about getting cute with a ccTLD: You run the risk of your website getting shut down if the government finds your content offensive. In 2010, vb.ly was seized by NIC.ly (the domain registry and controlling body for the Libyan domain space) because the content of the website was in violation of Libyan Islamic/Sharia Law. Now if they would only shut down Grammar.ly.

Silly Idea #3: Use .org for a For-Profit Business

I personally find it unethical for companies to use the .org domain extension, as I believe those should be available only for nonprofit organizations and NGOs. Using or squatting on a .org name is the bad-etiquette equivalent of illegally parking in a disabled parking space. Unfortunately, there are no restrictions on who can buy a .org domain.

Silly Idea #4: Domain Name = Trademark

Just because you own a domain name does not mean you own the trademark. The two are unrelated. I recently consulted for a client who spent $45,000 on a domain name only to find out later he could not legally call his company that name. Ouch! You should never purchase a domain name without first investigating if it is identical or similar to an existing trademark or service mark. Consult with a trademark attorney before you go too far in the domain process.

While researching trademarks for a client, I discovered the data analytics firm Company X, who bought its domain name in 2012, raised $9.3 million in funding, hired a few dozen employees, yet never bothered to trademark the name. Company X is a common name, and I'm not even sure it could get the trademark. That's incredibly foolish and naive. One day the company may receive a certified letter from the lawyer for a previously established Company X that claims that the domain name infringes on that company's federally registered trademark. It may issue an immediate cease-and-desist order prohibiting the use of the domain name and all references to the trademark. And it could insist that the company transfer the offending domain name to the original Company X and pay damages equal to all profits to date. Unfortunately, the above scenario is not uncommon. A third of the new business calls we get are from companies facing trademark infringement who are being forced to change their name—not to mention all of their branding—on everything from business cards to building signage.

Silly Idea #5: Don't Look before You Leap

Before you pounce on a domain name, make sure the words mashed together don't spell something unintentional, which is called a SLURL—a clever portmanteau of Slur + URL.

The dating website PlentyOfFish should have looked at their domain name more closely, as it also spells PlentyOffish, which is what some of my girlfriends refer to it as because of how off-putting some of the men can be in their messages.

Law firm Ferreth and Jobs didn't think this through when they bought ferrethandjobs.com. A few other mistakes:

penisland.com (PenIsland)

molestationnursery.com (MoleStationNursery)

therapistfinder.com (TherapistFinder)

michaelspornanimation (MichaelSpornAnimation)

lumbermansexchange (LumbermansExchange)

You'll find many more at slurls.com.

Domain names are important but should never be your primary focus when naming your company. Work on creating a memorable brand name, then start looking for a domain name. With the above tips, there's no reason why you can't have both.

CHAPTER 4

Your Brand Name Road Map

Creativity can't occur in a vacuum. Before you jump into the fun part—brainstorming names—it's essential to complete what's known as a *creative brief.* Think of it as the ingredients list of everything you need to cook up the perfect name: company/product history, information on your target audience, consumer insights, desired brand positioning, competitors' names, words to explore and avoid, and more. It may take a few days to complete the brief, but I promise that you'll be happy you put time into it. So will anyone who is helping come up with names. I will never start a project without one and absolutely insist that my clients complete one. The few times I've worked on projects without a brief, the names have been off strategy because I didn't have all the information.

The creative brief will help you define exactly what your brand is and what you want the name to communicate. Just as important, it will help you stay focused and prevent you from choosing the wrong name.

Keep in mind that you may write hundreds of words in your brief, but your name will be only one to three words and can't say everything.

I'm sharing the exact same brief with you that we give to our clients at Eat My Words. To help you get a better understanding of the kind of information you should write, the brief is filled out for a fictitious client, Cartwheel Kitchens. Study the questions and answers, and then recreate it for yourself with information about your own brand.

If you have multiple people involved in the naming process, make sure everyone agrees on what you write in your brief before you dive into naming. Getting all of the decision makers involved from the start is key to getting everyone to agree on a name.

Sample Creative Brief

Client: Cartwheel Kitchens

Project: Kids' Food Company Name

GOAL OF ASSIGNMENT
What do you want to accomplish?

Develop a brand name for a new snack food company that is better for you / better for the Earth. (Code name is Cartwheel Kitchens.)

IN A NUTSHELL
Sum it up in 140 characters or less.

Cartwheel Kitchens creates fun, better-for-you snacks that appeal both to health-conscious parents and kids with a taste for yummy treats.

BRAND POSITIONING
How do you want your brand to be positioned in the marketplace?

Cartwheel Kitchens is the preferred choice for moms seeking healthier and earth-friendly snacking options for their kids four to twelve years old because these snacks combine healthy ingredients with fresh-baked goodness and come in fun shapes and flavors that both moms and kids love.

CONSUMER INSIGHTS
Consumer insights reveal people's behaviors, as opposed to preferences. For instance, when naming an herbal tea brand, it helps to think beyond what tea drinkers like about herbal tea (e.g., flavor, fragrance, health benefits) and consider what circumstances lead them to enjoy their tea. It could be getting home after a long commute, relaxing with a book in their favorite chair, or sipping a cup before bedtime to help them get a restful sleep.

✦ Although eating healthier snacks in front of peers at or after school has gotten more acceptable (e.g., edamame), it is still not seen as cool by most kids.

✦ Most kids do not want to try anything that sounds healthy.

✦ Some kids post photos of their lunches via Instagram and Snapchat.

TARGET AUDIENCE
Who are the customers you want to reach?

✦ Moms, ages 25–45, with children, ages 4–12, households of 3+, income $45K+

✦ Kids, ages 4–12

COMPETITION
List your competitors so you know what you are up against and to help you steer clear of similar names, which could pose trademark conflicts.

Pepperidge Farm, Nabisco, Annie's, Plum Organics, Smart Snacks, Keebler, Moon Pie, Lunchables, Little Debbie, Dunkaroos, Teddy Grahams, Animal Crackers, Fig Newtons, Cheez-It, Cheese Nips, Ritz Bits Snacks, as well as makers of cookies, fruits snacks, pretzels, popcorn, and potato chips

DESIRED BRAND EXPERIENCES
The best names evoke a positive brand experience that makes a strong emotional connection, such as "This tastes great," "I will feel better," or "This is fun!"

Moms will think

✦ This company makes snacks I can feel good about feeding my kids.
✦ I trust this is good for my kids.
✦ I feel good giving my kids something healthier than they usually snack on.

Kids will think

✦ I know this is going to taste yummy.
✦ I am going to tell my friends about these.
✦ I love the fun shapes.

BRAND PERSONALITY
The 5–12 adjectives that best describe the tone and personality of your brand. (This exercise is much easier to do if you think of your brand as a person.)

Fun, playful, smart, approachable, likeable, lighthearted, kid friendly, energetic, modern, fresh, healthy

WORDS TO EXPLORE
List some words you may like to have in your new name.

Kitchens (e.g., Cartwheel Kitchens), Planet (e.g., Planet Snack / Snack Planet)

THEMES/IDEAS TO AVOID
Don't even think of going here:

Animals (our competitors have done this to death)
Acronyms (not kid-friendly)
Anything that sounds too young

WORDS TO AVOID
List any words you would not like to have in your new name.

Health/Healthy (repels kids)
Nature/Natural (everyone does this)
Green (dated)

DOMAIN NAME MODIFIERS
List modifier words that will help you secure a domain name, which may not be available as an exact match to your new name or may be out of your price range:

_____Snacks.com   Enjoy_____.com

Eat_____.com   KidsLove_____.com

NAME STYLE LIKES & DISLIKES
List 5 brand names that you collectively like the style of (and why).

1. Twizzlers (fun!)
2. Lunchables (fun, says "lunch," kid and parent friendly)
3. Jamba Juice (fun to say, energetic)
4. Pop Tarts (good visual imagery)
5. Plum Organics (cool name)

List 5 brand names that you collectively dislike the style of (and why)

1. Pedialyte (sounds like it's full of chemicals)
2. Nibs (too silly—no one wants to say this name out loud)

3. Toys "R" Us (grammatically incorrect)
   4. Little Debbie (very old fashioned)
   5. Oreo (doesn't mean anything)

ACID TEST FOR USING THE NEW NAME
Write how the new name would be used in a sentence.

_____ _____makes wholesome and healthy snacks that kids love because they taste good and come in fun shapes and flavors.

ALSO GOOD TO KNOW
List anything else you think would be important to the name development.

The snack aisle at the grocery store is a good place for inspiration. (Just don't go on an empty stomach.)

After you complete the creative brief, you and your team will have all the information you need to start brainstorming ideas.

CHAPTER 5

How to Be an Idea Machine

Brainstorming names is a blast when you know my secrets to coming up with great ideas. While counterintuitive, my method is highly effective, and you will be surprised and excited by how many good ideas you will generate and how quickly you will do it.

The Wrong Way to Brainstorm

Brainstorming meetings are terribly ineffective. Most corporate conference rooms have bare walls, fluorescent lighting, and, sadly, little mental stimulation. Group brainstorming is not process based. It's a mad free-for-all, where extroverts throw ideas at the wall and see what sticks. Introverts, who may have good ideas, may fear speaking up. Everyone sucks up to the boss. No one in the room has an objective filter for what makes a name good or bad. And if any name does get chosen, it's often a mediocre one that's met with the least resistance—instead of the *best* name,

Gathering friends over a bottle of wine (or two) is equally unproductive. Good ideas don't materialize out of thin air. Nor do they come from games of Drunken Scrabble, Ouija boards, or Magic 8 Balls.

The Right Way to Brainstorm

What is the ideal number of people for brainstorming name ideas? One: you. What is the optimal environment? In front of your computer. The single most powerful brainstorming tool is the Internet. Everything you need to come up with great name ideas is online.

When you brainstorm online, you'll find yourself clicking on unexpected links and going down all kinds of rabbit holes. You never know where a good idea will come from. As my extremely creative mother says, "The creative process is an idea orgy, where you can jump into bed with any enticing idea that comes along."

After nearly thirty years of working as an advertising copywriter and a namer, my personal brainstorming process is pretty organic, but for teaching purposes, I'll demonstrate how to do it in a structured manner, using some of my most lucrative online resources.

Before you get started, here are three helpful tips:

1. Open Your Mind

While you look up words, phrases, and images associated with what you're trying to name, let your mind become a playground. Bounce around. Turn things over. Put the unexpected together. Visualize. Fly overhead. Look at it from another angle. Take the lid off. Be fearless. There is no one there to shoot your ideas down, so go for it.

2. Write It Down

Write down all your name ideas. Even those that don't feel exactly right. They may later inspire you with a real zinger. When I create a list of names, I divide them into categories: Spot On, Maybe, and Sparks. By sharing these with my naming team, they can build off of my ideas and often turn the Sparks into fire.

3. Have Your Creative Brief Handy

Before you dive in, make sure you have written a detailed creative brief (as shown in the previous chapter). This background information and naming strategy will be your ingredients list. It helps to print out your brief to jot down ideas.

Let the Fun Begin!

To demonstrate the brainstorming process, I have recreated the online ideation exercises I performed to name a frozen yogurt franchise. Here are some key details from the creative brief and calls with the client. As you read this, imagine yourself going through this process for your own name.

GOAL OF ASSIGNMENT:
Develop a name for a new healthy, low-fat, frozen yogurt franchise. It will serve two flavors: green tea and tart. The first store will be in Utah. The client wanted to name it Zenyo or Swayo. (Yikes!)

TARGET AUDIENCE:
Primary—Teenagers
Secondary—Everyone else

BRAND PERSONALITY:
Hip, fun, cool

CONSUMER INSIGHTS:
Utah teens are not as square as you may think. Teens want to socialize outside of school and church.

BRAND EXPERIENCES:

Kids will think

- ✦ I will look cool if I'm seen here.
- ✦ This is a fun place to go with my friends.
- ✦ The name is so cool, I want to buy the T-shirt.

WORDS TO AVOID:

- ✦ Pink, or any color
- ✦ Berry, or any fruit

THE WARM-UP — LIST 12 WORD SPARKS

Before you jump onto your computer to look for ideas, write down at least a dozen words related to the brand or brand experiences. (You should be able to get a lot of these from your creative brief.) This word association exercise is not meant to be a list of names, just sparks to fuel your search for the perfect name.

For the frozen yogurt franchise, I wrote down these twelve words:

Cold	Skinny	Tart	Treat
Eat	Cool	Soft	Yo
Sweet	Chill	Tasty	Yummy

Next, choose one word from the above list. In this case, I've selected *cold*. (You'll later repeat all of these exercises using the remaining eleven words.)

Mine the Online Goldmine

There are countless places to get name ideas and inspiration online. These are some of my favorites. Be sure to try all of the tools and techniques below, as each one will yield many different ideas.

Open the Thesaurus Treasure Chest

Begin your online brainstorming on a thesaurus website, where you can find a jackpot of synonyms and related words. My go-to one is Thesaurus.com. Here are some of a few of the dozens of words I found when I searched for *cold*:

Bitter	Arctic	Nippy
Snowy	Chill	Polar
Wintry	Goose Bumps	Shivery

Let's take a closer look at the results:

Arctic — could be something there

Bitter — This would make an excellent edgy and fun name, especially because one of the two flavors is tart and bitter.

Chill — a little dated, even for Utah

Goose Bumps — I love the name Goosebumps (spelled as one word) for this frozen yogurt store. It's unexpected, and teenage love is all about goose bumps, so it works on two levels.

Nippy — funny, but no

Polar — The word on its own is dull, but *Polarize* would be fun because it has the double meaning of the two flavors being so polarizing.

Snowy — not a good name, but it leads me to my next brainstorming resource

Shivery — no, but there could be something with Shiver, which makes a nod to teen love, like Goosebumps

Wintry — weird word but *Winter* could be fun to play with

Of course not every word in the results is going to be the name, yet there are some excellent candidates:

Bitter

Goosebumps

Polarize (inspired by the word Polar)

Shiver (inspired by the word Shivery)

While the other words aren't ideal as names, they definitely spur more ideas. For instance, *Snowy* makes me think of building snowmen, which brings me to my next go-to brainstorming tool . . .

Supercharge Your Imagination with Images

A picture says a thousand words. And many of those words can inspire awesome names, which is why I always do image searches to fuel my creativity.

Inspired by *Snowy*, I point my browser to images.google.com and type "snow fun" into the search field. Immediately I see photos of kids building snowmen, having snowball fights, making snow angels, and flying down snow banks on saucers. Snow Angel could be a fun name, although I think the teens in Utah would love to shed their angelic image.

Next I type "snow sports" and get an array of photos of people having fun on skis, snowboards, inner tubes, sleds, toboggans, mountain bikes, and snowmobiles. I also see photos of a naked guy sitting on a slide at a snow-blanketed playground, two golden retrievers humping in the snow, and what appears to be a member of the Swedish Bikini Team, gliding down a bunny slope in a skimpy two-piece bathing suit. Note: If you are in a cubicle or at a café and don't have Google SafeSearch turned on, be warned that you may be exposed to these kinds of unexpected images, which can appear in the most innocuous searches. Professional stock photo websites such as istockphoto.com and gettyimages.com are also fantastic places to get ideas. I personally like to use Google because the amateur photos are more fun and it's endlessly entertaining.

The photos of the skiers and snowboarders are the catalyst for my next idea. . . .

Comb through Glossaries of Terms

Every sport has its own lingo of fun words and phrases. You can find pages and pages of them online by searching for "glossaries," "lingo," "vernacular," "jargon," "dictionaries," "thesaurus," "terms," "words," or "slang," which are essentially the same thing but will turn up different results in searches. Be sure to experiment with some of these.

Back to the frozen yogurt names. My image search of snow sports has inspired me to look up glossaries of lingo for snowboarding and skiing, two very popular sports in Salt Lake City, where the first location of the frozen yogurt store will be. I search Google for "snowboarding lingo" and hit the jackpot at gnu7.wordpress.com/snowboarding-lingo:

> If you're going to be a snowboarder, you have to talk like one! Here's a crash course in some common rider lingo. . . .

Here are some of the words and definitions I found on the first page of this website.

Shreddin' The Gnar — riding the terrain (Basically it's a really cool way to say, "We're going snowboarding.")

Chatter — when the board shakes because of the rough terrain (usually occurs when riding on an edge)

Yard Sale — a fall where someone's equipment falls off

Taco — a kind of fall where your body folds over a rail or box creating a taco shape

Reviewing the terms, the one that jumps out at me as being a fantastic name is Chatter. This is a rich word because it has so many layers of meaning. To snowboarders, it's lingo for a shaky board, but customers don't need to know that to appreciate the other meanings. *Chatter* implies cold (chattering teeth) and teens chattering with each other, which taps into the frozen yogurt store's desire to be the new place for teens to socialize (chatter) with each other. I add it to the list.

You can spend hours looking through glossaries to find ideas for names. Remember to try different keyword combinations while searching, such as *glossaries, jargon, terms, slang*, and *dictionaries*. While many of the terms that show up in glossaries will have the curse of knowledge and may be too *insider* for a name, you will usually find gems like *Chatter* that work regardless of whether someone knows the glossary meaning.

Glossaries are also helpful if you're searching for metaphorical names. For instance, if you were naming something fast, like a microchip, by thinking of other things that are fast (e.g., race car driving) and looking in those glossaries, you would find a lot of words and phrases that evoke speed.

Dictionaries Have More Than Just Definitions

You might be wondering why I would go to a dictionary website because, after all, everyone knows what *cold* means. However, dictionaries are deep wells of ideas. The one I like best is *The Free Dictionary* (thefreedictionary.com), which provides much more than definitions. It's also a thesaurus and an excellent source for phrases and idioms. I type in the word "cold" and get a mile of results and name ideas. Since there are 2,710 words for that entry, I'll simply give you the most fruitful and fun highlights of the definitions and phrases I found, some of which would make interesting names. Others, not so much.

DEFINITIONS OF COLD

Sexually unresponsive or frigid

Lacking emotion; objective (cold logic)

Marked by or sustaining a loss of body heat (cold hands and feet)

So intense as to be almost uncontrollable (cold fury)

Dead

PHRASES FOR COLD

common cold	cold sore
Cold War	cold feet
cold shoulder	in cold blood

Sometimes Clichés Are *Good*

Clichés—common phrases, such as Eat My Words—are some of the best sources for names. I typically find some unexpected ideas at clichesite.com. And even if I don't, it's always good for a laugh. Here are some results I got when I typed in "cold":

a cold heart	cold turkey
cold as a witch's tit	stone cold sober
cold as ice	to get cold feet

While most everything above isn't right for a name, *stone cold sober* could be shortened to *Cold Sober*, which I think is a funny name for a teen hangout in Utah. I add it to the list.

Go Googlestorming!

In addition to image searching, there are a myriad of other ways to utilize Google for brainstorming, or, as I call it, *Googlestorming*.

Continuing to explore the word *cold*, I type "coldest places on earth" into the search field. The first result looks promising: http://www.mnn.com/earth-matters/climate-weather/photos/7-of-the-coldest-places-in-the-world-to-live/bone-chilling.

7 of the coldest places in the world to live

Winter is here and it seems like a good time to look at some of the insanely cold places where people actually live.

I have no idea what mnn.com is, but am delighted to discover it is Mother Nature Network. What a fun name. I begin reading about bone-chilling places I have never heard of, can't pronounce, and will never be on my bucket list of places to go. (One of the best things about brainstorming online is learning about so many different things I would otherwise not know.)

First on the list is Verkhoyansk, Russia, which is 1,500 miles south of the North Pole and has "1,434 hardy residents who carve out a living in the deep Siberian wilderness." The word

Siberian jumps out at me. *Siberia* is a funny word that would make a super name for the frozen yogurt store. It implies cold. And considering that Utah is a kind of Siberia (removed from the rest of the population), it's just the type of self-deprecating name that teens would love. "Mom, I'm going to Siberia with my friends." Cool.

A little further reading on Mother Nature Network causes me to stumble across Yakutsk, Russia, which you may have heard of from playing the board game Risk. I learn that Yakutsk is known as the coldest city in the world and that "the world's coldest temperature outside of Antarctica was recorded not far from Yakutsk." I love the word *Antarctica*, because it's similar to Siberia in that it seems like another world and is unexpected and fun. I add it to the list and continue scouring the text for name ideas.

While I don't find any names on par with Siberia and Antarctica, I do learn that Hell, Norway, has gained notoriety for the combination of its name and subarctic temperatures. Hell freezes over, on average, a third of the year, running from December through March.

Pop culture references make great names because they are familiar. I named a janitorial company Eat My Dust, which was the name of a campy race car movie in the 70s. The name always gets a smile, even from people too young to remember the movie.

Movie Title Madness

Continuing with the exploration of the word *cold*, my next Google search term is "cold movies." I see that Populist.com has a list of the "Top 10 Freezing Cold Movies." (Thank you to everyone who creates lists like these. I love you.) In the top ten, I see *Nanook of the North*, *Dr. Zhivago*, and *Fargo*. These are great movies, but not great names for a yogurt store. On the same search, I see a freaky picture of Jack Nicholson in *The Shining*, which I then discover is available as a snow globe on Etsy. Are we having fun yet?

Breeze through Some Book Titles

Unlike business and product names, which are protected under trademark law, one cannot trademark a book title. That makes books ripe sources of ideas. (Don't try to use Harry Potter, though—that's a whole franchise unto itself.)

An Amazon search of book titles that contain the word *cold* shows 36,364 results. Of course I don't plan to go through all of these, but I look at the first few pages. To speed up the skimming process, I limit the results to "images." This way, I just see the book covers. Many titles—*In Cold Blood, Cold Fusion*, and *The Cold War*—have turned up in my other searches. But there are some new ideas, too:

> *Cold Comfort Farm* (Cold Comfort would be a nice name.)
>
> *Cold Hearted* (playful)
>
> *Biting Cold* (fun — *Biting* is a word I liked from the thesaurus search that I thought would be good paired with another word. This one works.)

We've covered books. Now let's move on to music.

Tune into iTunes

As with book titles, song titles (as well as album titles and band names) can't be trademarked and are up for grabs when it comes to brand names. And song titles make super sticky names because, just like the songs themselves, they get stuck in our head. A song-inspired brand name that I love is the car-sharing company Getaround. Every time I hear or see that name, that classic Beach Boys song starts playing in my head: "Round round get around, I get around, yeah." One of my favorite song-inspired names was for a chili pepper–infused brownie. I did an iTunes search for words related to heat. The word *burn* turned up the song made famous by Elvis Presley, "Burning Love." My mind immediately went to the catchy lyrics, "Hunka hunka burning love." I knew this would be a love-at-first-sight flavor name—Hunka Hunka Burning Love—made everyone smile.

A song search at the iTunes Store reveals these "cold" titles and band names:

Coldplay (fun!)

"Funky Cold Medina" (makes me laugh, but I'm not sure if teens would know this song. Plus, since Medina also happens to be a Muslim holy city, it might not play well in Utah.)

"Cold as Ice" (nope)

"Stone Cold Bitch" (uh, no)

Tip: Sort songs by popularity, as those will be the ones people know and have emotional connections with.

By now, I've exhausted the word *cold* and have come up with more than a dozen excellent name ideas.

Could you have come up with all of the above names by sitting in a sterile conference room staring at a white board? Doubtful. And you wouldn't have seen a random picture of two dogs humping in the snow. Just sayin'.

Next, I will repeat this process with the other eleven words on the initial list (eat, treat, cool, etc.) plus all of the new ones I came up with along the way. This process can take weeks (especially after trademark screens eliminate a lot of them), but it always yields more than a hundred name ideas. Come up with at least a few dozen names, as many will get eliminated during trademark screening. You never want to fall in love with just one name.

The Chosen Name

I came up with the winning name while doing an image search for "eat frozen yogurt," which led me to a lot of photos of plastic spoons in yogurt, which immediately made me think of the phrase "Spoon me." You never know where a great idea will come from.

The name Spoon Me perfectly fit the brand personality of "hip, fun, and cool." And it aced the SMILE & SCRATCH Test.

There are more than a dozen Spoon Me locations in North America. The company attributes a lot of its success to the name because it has such great legs. Before one of the stores opens, the "coming soon" sign says, "Spooning Soon." Door signage playfully cautions, "No Shirt, No Shoes, No Spoon." In Utah, the "Spooning Hours" warn, "No Spooning on Sunday." Interiors and branded merchandise feature evocative slogans like, "If you love me, Spoon Me," and "Shut up and Spoon Me." And restrooms are graffitied with famous movie slogans with a fun twist, such as "Yo Adrian, let's Spoon" and "You had me at Spoon Me." How many T-shirts would they have sold if they had called themselves Zenyo or Swayo?

Of course teens love the name Spoon Me, and surprisingly, the older Mormon couples—who we thought might be offended—find it sweet and endearing because spooning (with your clothes on) is seemingly innocent. Forking, however is a different matter.

ADDITIONAL FREE ONLINE BRAINSTORMING TOOLS
IdiomConnection.com

Wordoid.com

RhymeZone.com

Wordnik.com

Visuwords.com

CHAPTER 6

12 Rules for Building Consensus

Over the years, I have developed twelve rules for reviewing names when there are multiple decision makers involved. I promise you will have much more success finding *the* name if you follow these guidelines rather than trying to randomly choose the best names.

Before you distribute the list, write a sentence or two of rationale next to each name to help sell it in. At the top of the list, show how the name might be used in a sentence. For example:

_____ _____ makes wholesome and healthy snacks that kids love because they taste good and come in fun shapes and flavors.

12 Rules for Reviewing Your Names

Rule 1 Have people initially review the list of names *independently*, as opposed to in a group. This process allows decision makers on the team to freely express which names they like individually without the trepidation that can occur during group presentations. By giving team members the confidence to fearlessly say what names they like, you also eliminate the pressure for people to echo what the boss likes. This way, no good names go unnoticed and everyone's opinions are heard.

Rule 2 The essential question to ask yourself when reviewing the names is *not,* Do I like it? which is subject to personal bias. The better question to ask is, Is it right? which is much more objective and effective.

Rule 3 Refrain from negative comments. You will have greater success finding a name everyone can agree on if you focus strictly on what works. Negative comments are never helpful in building consensus.

Rule 4 Keep in mind that a name can't say everything—it can hint at what your brand does or highlight a positive brand experience but should not be expected to say it all.

Rule 5 For a better review experience, print out the list to review on paper instead of viewing it online. Read it multiple times, top to bottom and bottom to top. Give yourself a few days to let all the names sink in.

Rule 6 As tempting as it is, do not share your list with outsiders and ask for their opinions on SurveyMonkey. Asking people what they think or to vote for their favorite name shows a lack of confidence. They are not experts on your brand. You are. They are not knowledgeable about what makes a great name. You are. (If you have read this book!) Imagine if Richard Branson had asked others to weigh in on the name Virgin. It never would have flown. Trust yourself on what feels right to you. When you ask your friends and family, "What do you think of this name?" they interpret it as an invitation to criticize. It's better just to tell people, "We're excited to announce our new name . . ." Please trust me on this. If you ask everyone to chime in, you will end up with a mediocre name that met with the least resistance rather than the very best name.

Rule 7 Keep in mind that your name will rarely appear naked—it will usually appear in context with your logo on a website or within your sales materials. A good way to review company names is to imagine each one on your caller ID, name badge, store sign, website, or business card. Imagine product names on the product, a sales sheet, or on the shelf.

Rule 8 Don't be afraid to be different. The best names are often the ones that are unfamiliar. Think back to the first time you heard the name Google. Did you love it? No. Do you love it now? Most likely. A little discomfort is a good thing at first—it means you are doing something that people haven't seen before.

Rule 9 Refrain from looking up domain names this early in the process. If you can't resist, do not eliminate names that don't have the pure domain dot-com name available (unless it is a competitor's website). It's perfectly acceptable to add a modifier word (e.g., Tesla uses TeslaMotors.com) or to create a memorable phrase (e.g., Peanut Butter & Co. uses ILovePeanutButter.com).

Rule 10 Each reviewer should select at least ten names from the list.

Rule 11 Don't fall in love with any one name until after you have conducted trademark screens. Expect 30–50 percent of the names you come up with to already be in use or pose conflicts. As a rule of thumb, the hipper the industry, the harder it is to trademark a cool name. Ad agencies, design firms, and gaming companies are very clever, which make those areas extremely challenging for new names. More conservative businesses, such as finance and insurance, have plenty of room for cool names but are completely saturated with pedestrian names.

Rule 12 Have fun! Collect and sort the name lists to see where there is consensus. Then meet as a group to discuss the attributes of the top contenders, choose and rank your top five, and start the trademark screening process.

Don't Use Focus Groups

Just as I don't recommend asking your friends and family for their opinions on your names, I strongly discourage focus-group testing. Asking a group of strangers what names they like is asking for trouble. Without fail, a focus group will collectively water down name choices to the safest name instead of the strongest name.

Here are ten brand names that I believe would have been killed if they were presented to focus groups and what I imagine some people might have said:

Fossil	"Dirty old relic, brittle."
Lush	"An alcoholic."
Coach	"The worst place to sit in an airplane, angry guy with a whistle."
Shady Eyewear	"Sounds untrustworthy."
Skinny Cow	"Implies that if I buy this ice cream, I am fat."
The Body Shop	"Makes me think of a greasy auto body place."
True Religion	"Blasphemous!"

MAC Cosmetics	"Makes me think of cheeseburgers and computers."
Spoon Me	"Leads to teen pregnancy."
Banana Republic	"Disparaging, belittling."
Opium Perfume	"Drugs are illegal."

Congratulations!

By now you should be well on your way to having an awesome name. You have all of the tips, tools, and resources you need to create brand names that make people smile instead of scratch their head. And just as important, you have everything you need to talk a coworker, boss, or colleague out of a bad name and convince them not to give up if an exact-match domain name isn't available.

I would love to hear about new brand names created as a result of reading this book. Please feel free to share your story with me. I may write about you in my blog or the next edition of this book.

Alexandra Watkins
awesome@eatmywords.com
Twitter: @eatmywords

CHAPTER 7

Pros and Cons

After reading this book, you may be tempted to change your name. While I can't advise you without knowing your exact situation, I can share the pluses and minuses of name changes.

One concern you may have is that your customers know you by your current business name and won't be able to find you if you change it. While that may have been the case twenty years ago, now with email, website redirects, blog posts, and social media tools, it's now easy to keep your customers in the loop. In Chapter 1, I wrote about high-energy public relations pro Lynette Hoy, who after years of using her own name, "Lynette

Hoy PR," changed it to the more evocative Firetalker PR. Her only regret? Not doing it sooner. It's never too late to change your name.

Pros of Changing Your Name

✦ You can refresh your entire brand at the same time.

✦ You will save time (and save face) not having to explain or apologize for your difficult name.

✦ You will have an excellent reason to get in touch with past and current customers—to tell them about your new name.

✦ Chances are you have many more years in business ahead of you than behind you.

✦ You have thousands of future customers who don't know your current name and will know you only by your new name. (A good way to imagine this is if you're a married woman who hasn't used her maiden name in years. Think of all the people in your life who know you by your married name and how few know you by your maiden name.)

Cons of Changing Your Name

✦ You've had it for years and are emotionally attached to it.

✦ It may be difficult to get everyone in the company on board.

✦ The person who came up with it may get hurt feelings.

✦ It can be expensive to print new materials and signage.

✦ You may have to acknowledge that your previous name didn't pass the SMILE & SCRATCH test.

✦ You may have to get your tattoo removed.

Here are some successful name changes that we've done for clients:

Challenge: Jazz organization whose name didn't strike a chord with their members.
Original Name: Rhythmic Concepts Inc. (RCI)
New Name: Living Jazz

Challenge: Luxury goods website whose name sounded more like a mail order catalog than designer merchandise.
Original Name: Peach Direct
New Name: Venue

Challenge: Organization for high-level women execs whose name was a mouthful, even as an acronym.
Original Name: Forum for Women Entrepreneurs & Executives (FWE&E)
New Name: Watermark

Challenge: Business collaboration software whose descriptive name didn't stand out in the cloud crowd.
Original Name: CaptureToCloud
New Name: LiveHive

Challenge: Big data company whose confusing name was difficult for customers to pronounce and spell.
Original Name: uCirrus
New Name: Argyle Data (They find diamonds in data patterns.)

Challenge: Specialty grade coffee brand that hires ex-offenders. (While the name Second Chance works as the company name, consumers thought the beans were recycled.)
Original Name: Second Chance
New Name: I Have a Bean

Challenge: Personalized physical therapy platform with a name that needed a little rehab.
Original Name: Respondesign
New Name: Respond Well

RESOURCES

The How Awesome Is Your Name Self-Assessment Tool

Whether you want the confidence to move forward with a brand name or need to get a professional opinion to show your boss that his or her name idea is problematic, this professional assessment and printable report will tell you the truth about your name: the good, the bad, and the ugly. Fun and interactive, the detailed evaluation covers what you learned in the book and links to sites to check trademark availability, slang definitions, and translations in up to 30 languages.

This online companion product is available at:

www.bkconnection.com/ismynameawesome

Trademarking

Trademark screening is the most painful part of the naming process, yet it must be done. Do not skip this step. Protecting your name is critical. Those companies who don't trademark their name can lose it, which is incredibly costly and embarrassing.

When you register your name as a trademark, you can stop competitors from using or misappropriating your very same business name and anything that is confusingly similar to it.

What's the Big Deal about Having the Same Name?

Look up your own first and last name on Google or Facebook and see whom you share it with. Chances are, you would not want to be confused with those people. (Especially if you find yourself more attractive than them, which I'm sure you are.) They could be known scam artists, deadbeat dads, or convicted criminals.

I am horrified that people who type my name into Google Images see a frightful mug shot of a woman with very bad acne and a terrible bleach job who has been arrested twice for second-degree child neglect. If someone hadn't met me in person, they could be confused and think that was me. Yikes! It's bad enough to share a first and last name with someone you don't want to be confused with, but can you imagine sharing your brand name with a company or product that was totally undesirable? You would never want anyone to mistake your brand for that brand. That's why protecting your name is so important.

We had to kill a fantastic name we came up with for an Indonesian street food restaurant—Jakarta Jones—when a Google search revealed that a man with the same name had just been arrested a few hours earlier. Luckily we had an equally great runner-up, which is what our client is now using: Rickshaw Republic. (Oops, I forgot to Google "Rick Shaw.")

DIY Trademark Searches

Before you pay to have your names screened professionally, do some initial searching on your own. The easiest way to do this is with Google, looking for other brands with the same or a similar name. (If they are the same or in related areas, take them off your list.) For instance, if you were naming a web design firm, you would want to search for any kind of similarly named business that offered web design. That would include companies engaged in advertising, marketing, branding, social media, and public relations.

Your next free search step should be at Trademarkia.com, where you can quickly look for similar names that are already registered trademarks. For best results, use the advanced search. I love this website because the interface is very simple and user friendly. Additionally, search the free government trademark database TESS at USPTO.gov. As you can imagine, because it's a government website, it's not quite as slick as Trademarkia but is an excellent resource.

While do-it-yourself searches on Google, Trademarkia, and TESS are no guarantee that your name is available, they will save you time and money by eliminating names that are already in use.

Professional Trademark Screening Services

Before you spend thousands of dollars to register your name through an attorney, I suggest you use a professional trademark screening service for preliminary screens, which will save you a lot of money. My go-to firm is Tessera Trademark Screening (tessera.bz). The fee is $100 for the first name screened and $30 for every name thereafter. Tessera performs thorough multi-level trademark-screening research using the following screening tools:

✦ General and technical dictionaries

✦ Atlases and geographic dictionaries

✦ Business directories

- US Federal and US State trademark registers
- International trademark registers
- Online Internet search engines
- Domain names
- Industry databases

Keep in mind that preliminary trademark screening is insufficient for legal opinion, so your next step is to take the names that survived the preliminary screen to a trademark attorney to undergo a full clearance search.

I have provided names of reputable trademark attorneys later in this resource section.

Protect Your Trademark to Prevent Genericide

Many people tell me that they want their brand name to become so familiar that people use it as a verb, such as Google. Be careful what you wish for. Sometimes well-known names are so familiar to us that they become synonymous with the products themselves and lose their trademark. Words including *aspirin, thermos,* and *escalator* were protectable trademarks that met the fate of genericide and became generic words that any competitor can use. Brand names such as Band-Aid, Kleenex, Spandex, Baggies, Xerox, Plexiglas, and Rollerblade have spent millions to stop and prevent others from using their names and tarnishing their reputations.

Be diligent in protecting your name, as Gerber is about its trademarked ONESIES®, which is commonly misused. The word is not allowed on eBay when describing infant bodysuits unless Gerber makes the item, and both eBay and Gerber are vigilant about it.

The International Trademark Association provides the following guidelines to avoid genericide:[*]

---

[*] Available at www.inta.org/INTABulletin/Pages/PracticalTipson AvoidingGenericide.aspx

✦ Use the generic name of the goods with the trademark (Q-Tips cotton swabs) (and, if your product is the first entrant, come up with a generic term for the product);

✦ Give proper notice of a registered trademark to consumers by using either: "Registered in U.S. Patent and Trademark Office" or "Reg. U.S. Pat. & Tm. Off." or the letter R enclosed within a circle, ®. 15 U.S.C. § 1111. For an unregistered mark, use TM;

✦ Distinguish the trademark from surrounding text by capitalizing the trademark, using a distinctive typeface, or at the very least, capitalizing the first letter of the trademark;

✦ Use the trademark as an adjective (KLEENEX tissues);

✦ Do not use the trademark as a noun (KLEENEX);

✦ Do not use the trademark in the plural (incorrect: buy two DR. PEPPERS; correct: buy two DR. PEPPER soda beverages);

✦ Do not use the trademark as a verb (incorrect—XEROX the document; correct—make a copy using a XEROX copier);

✦ Do not abbreviate the trademark or alter it in any way (use H&M and not H and M);

✦ Use the trademark on a line of products rather than a single product (NIKE, used on sneakers and clothing);

✦ Object to others' misuse of the trademark; and

✦ Educate the public, including individuals within the trademark owner's organization, distributors, dealers, and consumers, to ensure proper usage of the trademark. Misuse often occurs due to lack of education, not wrongful intent.

You can find much more about trademark law at USPTO.gov.

Logo & Identity Design

A professionally designed logo and identity materials will bring your name to life and add credibility to your name. That's why investing in a well-planned identity system from the start is important to the long-term success of your brand. Please do not try to save money by crowdsourcing the design of your logo or getting someone to do it cheap or free. You get what you pay for, and this is not something you should ever skimp on. Nothing cheapens a name like poor design.

More than just a logo, visual design includes colors, typography, and every element of your brand that will need visual design. This can consist of your

+ Website & app design
+ Social media sites
+ Presentations
+ Printed materials
+ Packaging
+ Business cards
+ Digital letterhead
+ Signage
+ Tradeshow booth design
+ T-shirts & promotional items

Strong Visual Branding Builds Buzz

Boxbee is an urban storage company that is experiencing the positive effects of good visual design. They recently dropped off some boxes for me. Instead of generic gray crates, these were bright yellow with the Boxbee logo stamped on the sides. When their delivery guys are wheeling a dolly of yellow boxes down the street, people stop to talk to them because the boxes catch their attention. And lots of people wave when they see the fun buzzing bee graphics on the delivery van.

I've listed a few design firms on the Service Providers page of the Resources section and hope you will consider using one of them. If you choose to find your own designer, keep in mind that, just as with naming, identity design is highly specialized and therefore requires a specialist. While a company may say it can do the job, you want the expertise to execute a visually striking identity program. So be cautious when entrusting your work to a web designer, printing company (e.g., Vista Print), or even a naming firm. (Would you want a podiatrist to perform heart surgery on you? Same thing.) Hire a professional design firm or graphic designer who has a portfolio full of beautifully cohesive identity systems, not just a few logos.

Image is everything.

Service Providers

None of these companies have paid me a fee or bribed me with cupcakes to be listed here.

TRADEMARK SCREENING
Tessera.bz
VanekLaw.com

COPYWRITERS
GinaColada.com
AbbyWords.com

TRADEMARK FIRMS
BedrockSF.com
OlinerLaw.com

SOCIAL MEDIA
JeffBullas.com
SocialAna.com

TRANSLATION SERVICES
TravelingBrand.com
BrandedTranslations.com

PRESENTATION DESIGN
WeAreVisual.com
BigFishPresentations.com

BRAND IDENTITY FIRMS
StudioMoon.com
JustCreative.com

WEB/DIGITAL DESIGN
GoodDogDesign.com
ShiriDesignStudio.com

ACKNOWLEDGMENTS

I am grateful to the many people who believed in me through-out my career and made this book come together.

I owe my deepest gratitude to my awesome mother, Joan Casale. Mom, I hit the genetic jackpot of creativity because of you. Thank you for letting me express my creative side from a young age and not freaking out when I painted my bedroom Pepto-Bismol pink. Thank you for supporting every risk I have ever taken and for being my best role model, biggest cheer-leader, unwavering supporter, and loyal friend. You have been a tremendous part of this book. I so appreciate your insightful ideas, creative contributions, and eagle-eyed proofreading. I am so lucky to have you as my mom, and I am proud to be your daughter. Lastly, thanks for giving me the awesome name of Alexandra, forty years before it became trendy.

Dad, thank you for your good genes, too. I inherited your business acumen and wish you could be here to share in my suc-cesses. Thank you for inspiring me to be a fearless traveler and for accompanying me in spirit on so many journeys around the world. You are forever in my heart and carry-on bag.

Steve Piersanti and the hard-working team at Berrett-Kohler Publishers—I am honored to be one of your authors. Thank you for making this process so fun and painless. I am especially grateful to Grace Ellen Miller, BK sales and marketing assistant, who discovered me while she was an intern, and to BK's editorial managing director, Jeevan Sivasubramaniam, who pushed me to write a book—something I never wanted to do before. Thank you for taking me under your wing and being a terrific mentor and motivator. Kat Engh, Kristen Franz, and Michael Crowley were also a dream to work with and I am so appreciative for all of the personal attention they gave me.

Thanks to the "dynamic duo," David Peattie and copyeditor Tanya Grove of BookMatters — I am grateful for your expertise and attention to detail — you truly live up to the name of your company.

My book reviewers, Kendra Armer, Pam Gordon, Jess Bruner, and Jenny Williams, gave me invaluable feedback. And my outside book advisors Andy Core, Tim Grahl, Pat Hanlon, and Ana Lucia Novak generously shared their collective wisdom with me. I'm also grateful for the help of Jane Poynter, Sophie-Charlotte Moatti, Joe Robinson, Cathy Bennett, Debbie Irwin, and Jennifer Strongin.

I could not have written a book and simultaneously kept my business running without an amazing team alongside me. Gina Sorrel, thank you for making every day at Eat My Words a piece of cake for the past seven years. I value our friendship as much as your talent and tenacity as our associate creative director. Major props to my rock-star namers: Ryan "Darth Namer" Parks, Jake Abrahamson, Katie Mills, Caroline Leavitt, Natalie Sanderson, and Emily Smith.

Of course there would not be a book at all if it weren't for my countless cool clients. Thank you for entrusting me to name your "babies," letting me share your stories, and for paying for my vacations.

Tracy Moon of StudioMoon first taught me the business of naming and identity design—thank you for the countless favors you have done for me, including designing the cover of this book. You are an amazing designer, teacher, and friend.

I am lucky to have the encouragement of so many people with unwavering faith in me: Victoria Watkins, Veronica Casale, Carol Garcia, George Landau, Gretchen Sunderland, Ed Rice, Marcia Kadanoff, Cindy Lee, Kris Bleything, Ron Werthmann, Jim Fox, Terry Joyce, Blake Middleton, Ellen Leanse, Nell Merlino, my fellow Make Mine a Million awardees. Thank you for being on my cheerleading squad.

Shout-outs to my fellow naming professionals who welcomed

me into the flock and have generously shared your knowledge and experiences: Anthony Shore, Steve Manning, Mark Gunnion, Nancy Friedman, Phil Davis, Steve Cecil, Deborah Schatten, and Amy Sherman. And my team of trademark sharks: Steve Price, Angela Wilcox, Leila Banijamali, and Liz Olaner—thanks for your help and legal expertise.

Dan and Chip Heath, thank you for writing "Made to Stick," inspiring the SMILE & SCRATCH Test, and being a fan of Eat My Words since the beginning.

Many other authors and business leaders have influenced me, including Richard Branson, Donny Deutsch, Barbara Corcoran, Robert Herjavac, Lori Greiner, Malcolm Gladwell, Dan Pink, Simon Sinek, Seth Godin, Scott Stratten, and Tom Rath. Thank you for your words of wisdom.

Props to the best Head Scratcher hunter ever, Robin Wolaner, and everyone who has ever sent me a bad name, fantastic name, or something funny or crazy to Tweet or put on our Facebook page. Good looking out.

Finally, thank you to everyone who reads this book. You are awesome.

Eat My Words
161 Gilbert Street, Loft 3
San Francisco CA 94103
Tel: (415) 552-7741
eatmywords.com

INDEX

ABOUT
EAT MY WORDS

Founded in 2005 by Alexandra Watkins, a former award-winning Ogilvy & Mather copywriter, Eat My Words (www.eatmywords .com) works with funded companies to create unforgettable brand names and taglines that make powerful emotional connections and generate revenue. While we started out naming things that make people fat and drunk, now we name everything from robots to racehorses.

Our namedropper clients include Disney, Microsoft, Adobe, Del Monte, Fujitsu, Frito-Lay, TaylorMade Golf, American Licorice Company, Turner Broadcasting, LPL Financial, Guthy-Renker, Hasbro, Safeway, and Wrigley.

Unlike naming agencies and branding firms who butcher the alphabet to create ridiculously contrived brand names that people can't pronounce, spell, or relate to, Eat My Words creates incredibly likable, catchy, creative names and taglines that make powerful emotional connections and create instant brand affinity.

We develop our names using the Eat My Words SMILE & SCRATCH test, our proven 12-step name evaluation method, which has been featured in the *Wall Street Journal* and *Inc.* This filter is based on our philosophy: a name should make you smile, instead of scratch your head.

Our love-at-first-sight consumer names include frozen yogurt franchise Spoon Me, robotic vacuum Neato, Colombian language school Gringo Lingo, and Denver's Church of Cupcakes. And B2B names that we've created include Altimeter Group, Tribewire, Lightbox Libraries, and Argyle Data.

Eat My Words is the only naming firm to successfully monetize a client's name through merchandise sales. Our names are so likeable that consumers want to show them off. You can find

Eat My Words' names on T-shirts, laundry bags, coffee mugs, beer growler jugs, baby clothing, tote bags, underwear, and booty shorts.

Located south of Twittertown and a stone's throw from Pinterest, Airbnb, Zynga, and Adobe, our office is tucked away in a quiet alley in San Francisco's SOMA neighborhood. Affectionately known as Candyland, it is full of wall-to-wall eye candy, including a sofa made out of stuffed animals, a 1950s diner booth (Alexandra's desk), and a retro pink fridge, where we store our "coolest" books. Our colorful digs have been featured in design books, magazines, and television shows, including "Ultimate Kitchens" on the Food Network and "Small Space, Big Style" on HGTV. You can see photos at www.eatmywords.com/about/our-digs.

ABOUT THE AUTHOR

Paul K. Benjamin, PKB Visions

Founder of naming firm Eat My Words, Alexandra Watkins is a recognized expert on brand names with buzz. An animated guest on TV news shows, she is frequently quoted in the press and has been featured in leading business publications, including the *Wall Street Journal*, *Inc.*, and *Entrepreneur*. Alexandra is a popular speaker at MBA programs and has been a guest presenter multiple times at the Stanford Graduate School of Business, San Francisco State University, and USF's School of Management and its alumni association. She has also presented to Procter & Gamble alumni, UnCollege, In-House Agency Forum, General Assembly, and many co-working spaces.

Alexandra first got hooked on naming when Gap hired her to create cheeky names for their first line of body-care products. Soon after, she broke into the business by talking her way into branding powerhouse Landor via a Match.com date. With her fresh, unconventional naming style, Alexandra soon became a go-to resource for countless branding and naming firms around the country. And Landor sent her enough business to open her own firm. Since then, she's generated thousands of names for snacks, software, sunscreen, social networking sites, sportswear, shoes, sugar scrubs, serums, and seafood. (And that's just the S's!) She's also named lots of things that make people fat and drunk, including a nationally recognized bacon cheeseburger (which, ironically, must remain nameless).

Prior to Eat My Words, Alexandra was an advertising copywriter, working at leading ad agencies up and down the West Coast, including five years at Ogilvy and Mather, where she helped launch Microsoft Windows and learned the language of Geek Speak. In the mid-nineties she jumped on the dot-com gravy train and rode it until it crashed in her SOMA backyard. Alexandra took the money and ran, spending a year in Australia, New Zealand, Bali, and Fiji. Upon her return, she discovered her passion for naming things and soon after started Eat My Words.

Alexandra gets her passport stamped as often as possible. She has eaten her way through forty-five countries on six continents where she's sunk her teeth into local delicacies, including barbequed squirrel in Tanzania, ostrich carpaccio in South Africa, stewed camel meat in Libya, and lobster marinara in Cuba. Her favorite food is Jif peanut butter, which she once survived on for two days on the remote island of Amantani in Lake Titicaca, Peru.

She is currently planning her next adventure.

Ask Alexandra

What is your favorite brand name ever?
Kryptonite, the industrial-strength bike locks.

Why do you have such a beef with the name Xobni?
It's not just that the name is hard to spell, pronounce, and understand. Years ago I sent Xobni a shiny Head Scratcher of the Year trophy, and they never sent a thank-you card.

Can I send you SMILE and SCRATCH names that I see?
Please do! Tweet good and bad names to @eatmywords.com.

I'm too busy to come up with a name on my own. How much do you charge?
Our fees vary wildly depending on the size of the client, number of decision makers, domain name needs, trademark class saturation, and fun factor. Some clients have paid us in trade with ice cream and chocolate, and others have forked over as much as $50K.

I want to work for you! How do I apply to be one of your namers?
If you think you have what it takes to work for Eat My Words, you can take our namer test at http://eatmywords.com/contact/dream-jobs. Please note that I do not review the submissions personally—my sous-chefs do that, and I see only the tests that get the thumbs-up from them.

Will you review my list of names for me?
While I'm happy to review your names, I have an expensive shoe habit to support, so I do not review names for free. My fee is $1000 to review up to ten names and provide professional feed-

back and creative direction. (If you tell me you've read my book, I will review more than ten names.)

Will you teach my company how to do this?
If you work in a large corporation and would like me to train the troops, you can have me come in for a Spilling The Beans corporate naming workshop where we will name a product in real time. More about those here: http://eatmywords.com/services/workshops

Do you do speaking engagements?
I love an audience, so if you have an event that you think would benefit from hearing me speak, please visit this page for more information: http://eatmywords.com/services/speaking/

Will you talk to my book discussion group?
Providing I'm having a good hair day, I am available to speak to your book discussion group or reading club via Skype, and may even come in person if you are in the Bay Area and will feed me. Shoot me an email at awesome@eatmywords.com.

Berrett–Koehler
Publishers

A community dedicated to creating
a world that works for all

Dear Reader,

Thank you for picking up this book and joining our worldwide community of Berrett-Koehler readers. We share ideas that bring positive change into people's lives, organizations, and society.

To welcome you, we'd like to offer you a free e-book. You can pick from among twelve of our bestselling books by entering the promotional code **BKP92E** here: http://www.bkconnection.com/welcome.

When you claim your free e-book, we'll also send you a copy of our e-newsletter, the *BK Communiqué*. Although you're free to unsubscribe, there are many benefits to sticking around. In every issue of our newsletter you'll find

- A free e-book
- Tips from famous authors
- Discounts on spotlight titles
- Hilarious insider publishing news
- A chance to win a prize for answering a riddle

Best of all, our readers tell us, "Your newsletter is the only one I actually read." So claim your gift today, and please stay in touch!

Sincerely,

Charlotte Ashlock
Steward of the BK Website

Questions? Comments? Contact me at bkcommunity@bkpub.com.

MIX
From responsible sources
FSC
www.fsc.org   FSC® C113845

Certified
Corporation
bcorporation.net